GCSE English Literature AQA Anthology

Place

The Study Guide
Higher Level

This book is a step-by-step guide to becoming an expert on the Anthology part of your GCSE English Literature exam.

It's got everything you need to know — annotated poems, key themes, exam advice and worked essays.

It's ideal for use as a classroom study book or a revision guide.

What CGP is all about

Our sole aim here at CGP is to produce the highest quality books — carefully written, immaculately presented and dangerously close to being funny.

Then we work our socks off to get them out to you — at the cheapest possible prices.

Contents

How to Use this Book 1

Section One — Poems from the Literary Heritage

London — William Blake 4
The Wild Swans at Coole — William Butler Yeats 6
The Prelude — William Wordsworth 8
Spellbound — Emily Brontë 10
Below the Green Corrie — Norman MacCaig 12
Storm in the Black Forest — D H Lawrence 14
Wind — Ted Hughes 16

Section Two — Contemporary Poems

The Blackbird of Glanmore — Seamus Heaney 18
A Vision — Simon Armitage 20
The Moment — Margaret Atwood 22
Cold Knap Lake — Gillian Clarke 24
Price We Pay for the Sun — Grace Nichols 26
Neighbours — Gillian Clarke 28
Crossing the Loch — Kathleen Jamie 30
Hard Water — Jean Sprackland 32

Section Three — Themes

Place 34
Nature 36
Memory 38
Sadness 39
Uncertainty 40
Relationships 41
Passion 42
Hope 43

Section Four — Poetry Techniques

Poetic Forms 44
Poetic Devices and Structure 45
Beginnings of Poems 46
Couplets and Last Lines 47
Rhyme and Rhythm 48
Use of the First Person 49
Imagery 50
Language Features 51
Irony 52
Mood 53

Section Five — The Poetry Exam

The Poetry Exam: Unit Two Overview 54
Sample Question 1 55
Planning 56
How to Answer the Question 57
Mark Scheme 58
Sample Question 2 59
How to Answer the Question 60
Sample Question 3 62
How to Answer the Question 63

Section Six — Controlled Assessment

The Controlled Assessment 64

Section Seven — How to Write an A* Answer

How to Write an A* Answer 68

Glossary 72
Index 74
Acknowledgements 76

Published by Coordination Group Publications Ltd.

Editors:
Edward Robinson, Hayley Thompson

Produced with:
Alison Smith, Peter Thomas, Nicola Woodfin

Contributors:
Caroline Bagshaw, Roland Haynes, Elisabeth Sanderson

With thanks to Laura Jenkinson and Katherine Reed for the proofreading and Jan Greenway for the copyright research.

ISBN: 978 1 84762 536 6

Groovy website: www.cgpbooks.co.uk
Jolly bits of clipart from CorelDRAW®
Printed by Elanders Hindson Ltd, Newcastle upon Tyne.

Based on the classic CGP style created by Richard Parsons.

Photocopying — it's dull, grey and sometimes a bit naughty. Luckily, it's dead cheap, easy and quick to order more copies of this book from CGP — just call us on 0870 750 1242. Phew!

Text, design, layout and original illustrations © Coordination Group Publications Ltd. 2010
All rights reserved.

How to Use this Book

This guide is for anyone studying the <u>Place</u> cluster of the AQA GCSE English Literature Poetry Anthology. You'll have to either answer an <u>exam question</u> on the poems, or write about them for your <u>controlled assessment</u> — your teacher will tell you which.

Sections One and Two are About The Poems

There are usually <u>two pages</u> about <u>each poem</u>. This is what the pages look like:

There's a nice picture of <u>the poet</u> and some info about their life.

Important or tricky bits of the poem are <u>highlighted</u> and <u>explained</u>.

Difficult words are defined in the <u>poem dictionary</u>.

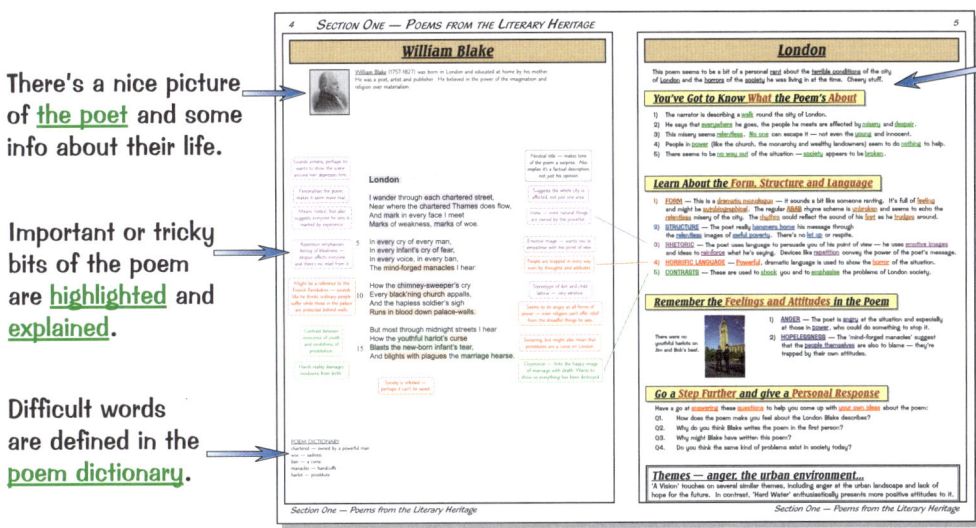

On the right-hand page there are <u>notes</u> about the poem. They include:

- what happens in the poem
- the <u>form</u>, <u>structure</u> and <u>language</u> the poet uses
- the <u>feelings</u> and <u>attitudes</u> in the poem
- a few questions asking you about <u>your feelings</u> on the poem.

If the poem's a bit of a <u>long one</u>, it'll be spread over <u>two pages</u>. One of these will be a <u>pull-out flap</u>. Don't panic. There are full instructions on what to do: THIS IS A FLAP. FOLD THIS PAGE OUT.

It's Really Important You Know Your Stuff

Whether you're doing the exam or the controlled assessment, you need to be really <u>familiar</u> with the poems.

1) You <u>won't notice</u> everything about a poem on <u>first reading</u>. Keep reading these poems over and over and <u>over again</u>.

2) If you notice something about a poem then <u>jot it down</u> — there's <u>no limit</u> to the number of <u>valid points</u> that could be made about these poems.

3) Make sure you have a go at <u>answering</u> those questions at the bottom of the right-hand page.

The questions are designed to make you <u>think for yourself</u> about the poems. You'll get <u>marks</u> in both the exam and the controlled assessment for giving <u>your own ideas</u> and <u>opinions</u> on the texts — it's called a <u>personal response</u>.

Nigel's first response to the poems wasn't all that positive.

How to Use this Book

You've got to make comparisons between the poems in your writing — so I've included two dead handy sections showing their similarities and differences. No need to thank me.

Section Three is About Themes

This section will help you make links between the themes presented in the poems — it'll give you loads of ideas of what to write about in your exam or controlled assessment.

A different theme is looked at on each page.

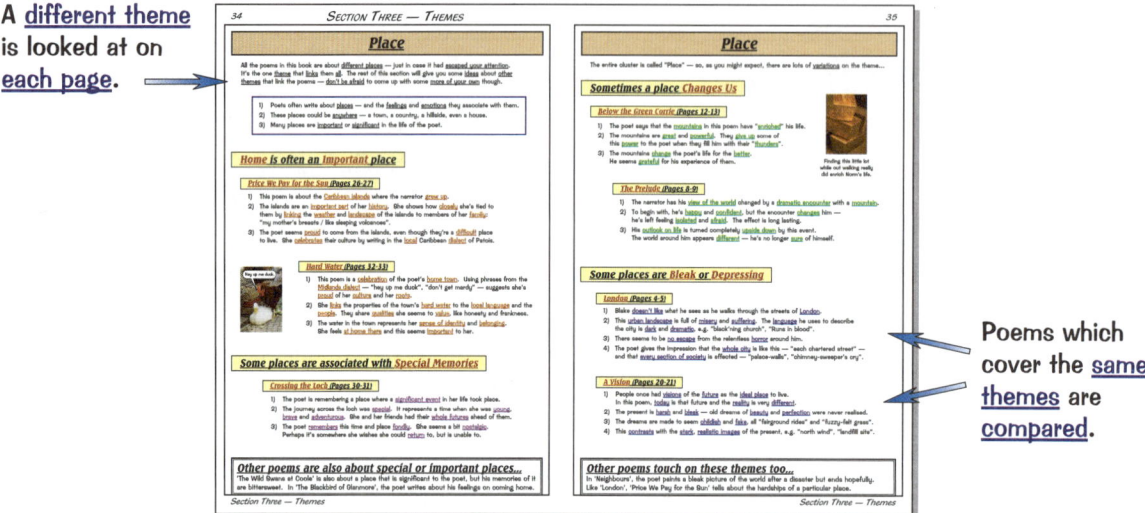

Poems which cover the same themes are compared.

Section Four is About Poetry Techniques

1) This section is all about form, structure and language.
2) It looks at how different poets use features like rhyme, rhythm and imagery to create effects — it's something the examiners are dead keen for you to understand and write about.

Each term is explained...

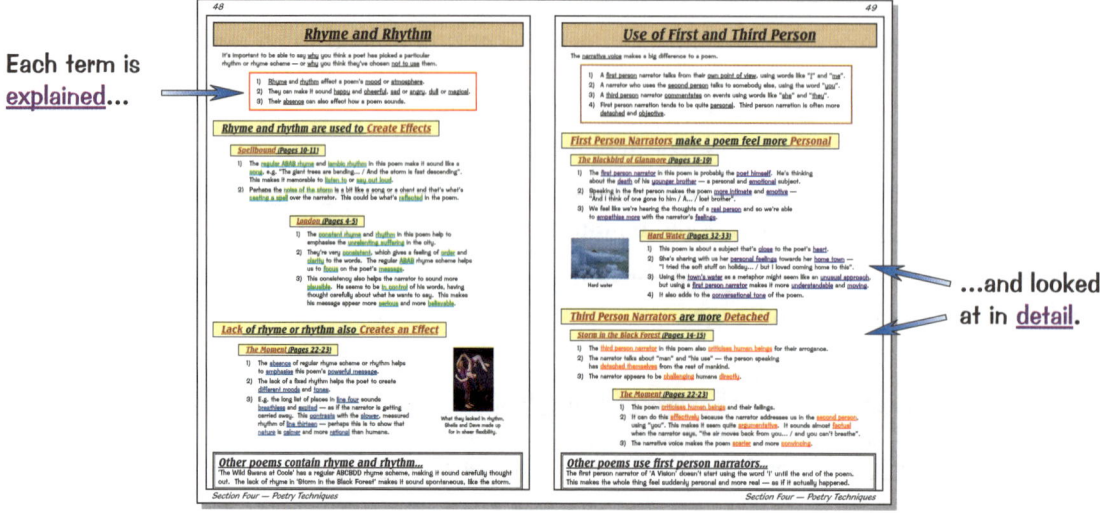

...and looked at in detail.

How to Use this Book

If you're studying these poems for the Unit 2 exam, then you need Section Five.
If you're doing these poems for your Unit 5 controlled assessment, look at Section Six.

Section Five Tells You What to Do in Your Exam

This is where you can find out exactly what's involved in your Unit 2: Poetry Across Time exam.

There are questions like the ones you'll get in the exam...

... and sample plans to show you different ways to plan your essay.

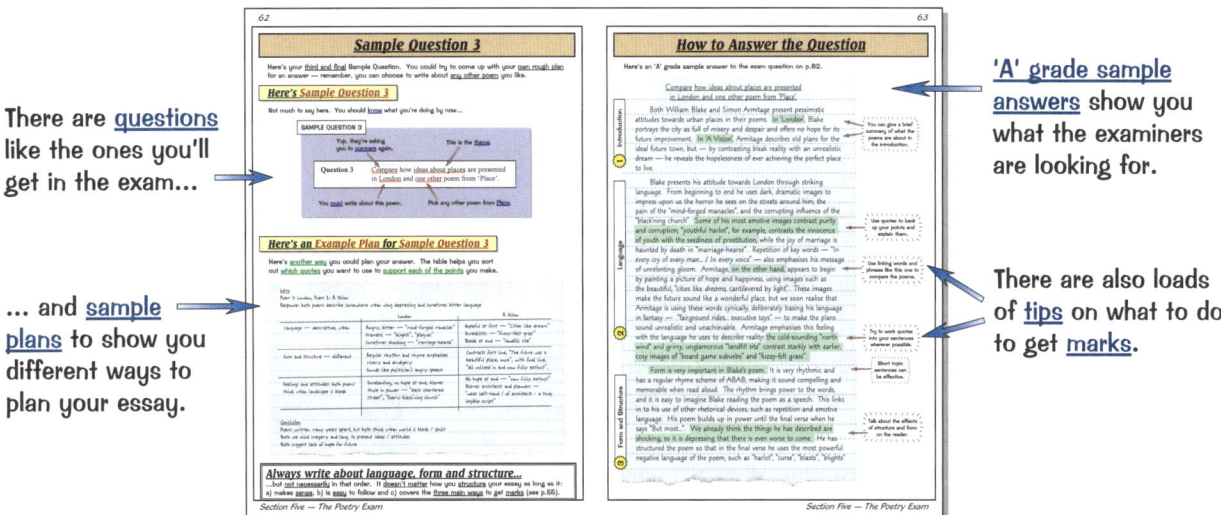

'A' grade sample answers show you what the examiners are looking for.

There are also loads of tips on what to do to get marks.

Section Six Tells You What to Do in Your Controlled Assessment

This section gives you the lowdown on the Unit 5: Exploring Poetry controlled assessment.

There are some example questions like the ones you'll be given, as well as...

...tips on planning and preparing for your assessment piece...

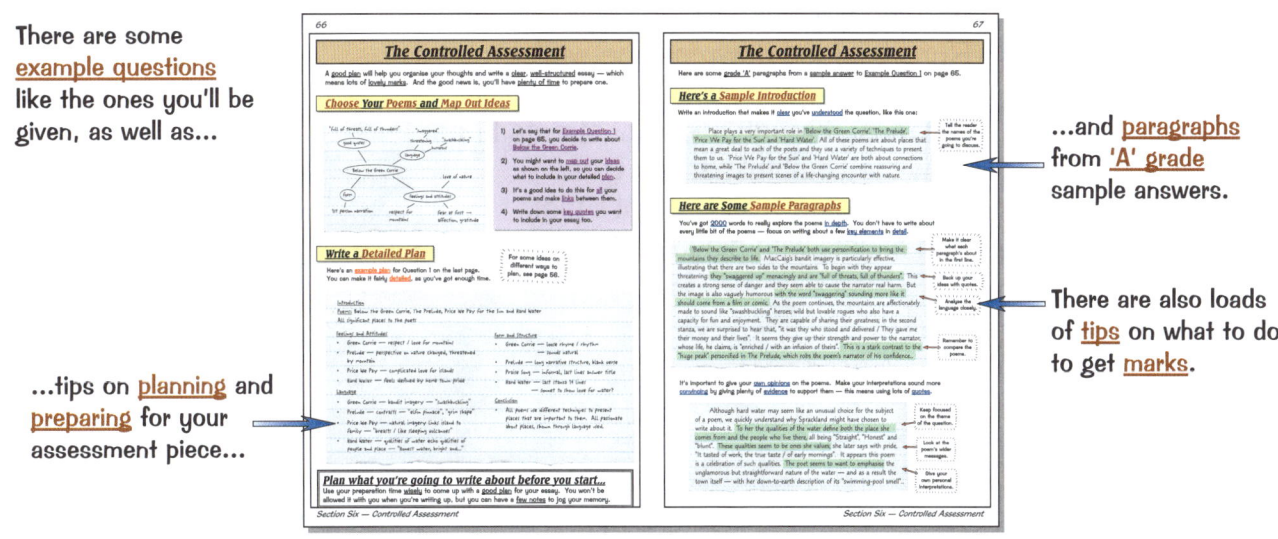

...and paragraphs from 'A' grade sample answers.

There are also loads of tips on what to do to get marks.

Section Seven Tells You How to Write An A* Answer

1) Whether you're aiming for an A* or not, this is a really useful section — there are tons of tips for how to improve your work.

2) It tells you how to get the highest marks and gives you loads of examples showing how to do it.

SECTION ONE — POEMS FROM THE LITERARY HERITAGE

William Blake

William Blake (1757-1827) was born in London and educated at home by his mother. He was a poet and artist who believed in the power of the imagination and religion over materialism.

- Sounds aimless — perhaps he wants to show the scene around him depresses him.
- Personalises the poem, makes it seem more real.
- Means 'notice', but also suggests everyone he sees is marked by experience.
- Repetition emphasises feeling of bleakness — despair affects everyone and there's no relief from it.
- Might be a reference to the French Revolution — sounds like he thinks ordinary people suffer while those in the palace are protected behind walls.
- Contrast between innocence of youth and sordidness of prostitution.
- Harsh reality damages newborns from birth.

London

I wander through each chartered street,
Near where the chartered Thames does flow,
And mark in every face I meet
Marks of weakness, marks of woe.

5 In every cry of every man,
In every infant's cry of fear,
In every voice, in every ban,
The mind-forged manacles I hear:

How the chimney-sweeper's cry
10 Every black'ning church appalls,
And the hapless soldier's sigh
Runs in blood down palace-walls.

But most through midnight streets I hear
How the youthful harlot's curse
15 Blasts the new-born infant's tear,
And blights with plagues the marriage hearse.

- Neutral title — makes tone of the poem a surprise. Also implies it's a factual description, not just his opinion.
- Suggests the whole city is affected, not just one area.
- Ironic — even natural things are controlled by the powerful.
- Emotive image — wants you to empathise with his point of view.
- People are trapped in every way, even by thoughts and attitudes.
- Image of dirt and child labour — very emotive.
- Seems to be angry at all forms of power — even religion can't offer relief from the dreadful things he sees.
- Swearing, but might also mean that prostitutes are a curse on London.
- Oxymoron — links the happy image of marriage with death. Wants to show us everything has been destroyed.
- Society is infested — perhaps it can't be saved.

POEM DICTIONARY
chartered — rented out or organised for business purposes
woe — sadness
ban — a curse
manacles — handcuffs
harlot — a prostitute

London

This poem seems to be a bit of a personal rant about the terrible conditions of the city of London and the horrors of the society he was living in at the time. Cheery stuff.

You've Got to Know What the Poem's About

1) The narrator is describing a walk round the city of London.
2) He says that everywhere he goes, the people he meets are affected by misery and despair.
3) This misery seems relentless. No one can escape it — not even the young and innocent.
4) People in power (like the church, the monarchy and wealthy landowners) seem to do nothing to help.
5) There seems to be no way out of the situation — society appears to be broken.

Learn About the Form, Structure and Language

1) FORM — This is a dramatic monologue — it sounds a bit like someone ranting. It's full of feeling and might be autobiographical. The regular ABAB rhyme scheme is unbroken and seems to echo the relentless misery of the city. The rhythm could reflect the sound of his feet as he trudges around.
2) STRUCTURE — The poet really hammers home his message through the relentless images of awful poverty. There's no let up or respite.
3) RHETORIC — The poet uses language to persuade you of his point of view — he uses emotive images and ideas to reinforce what he's saying. Devices like repetition convey the power of the poet's message.
4) HORRIFIC LANGUAGE — Powerful, dramatic language is used to show the horror of the situation.
5) CONTRASTS — These are used to shock you and to emphasise the problems of London society.

Remember the Feelings and Attitudes in the Poem

There were no youthful harlots on Jim and Bob's beat.

1) ANGER — The poet is angry at the situation and especially at those in power, who could do something to stop it.
2) HOPELESSNESS — The 'mind-forged manacles' suggest that the people themselves are also to blame — they're trapped by their own attitudes.

Go a Step Further and give a Personal Response

Have a go at answering these questions to help you come up with your own ideas about the poem:
Q1. How does the poem make you feel about the London Blake describes?
Q2. Why do you think Blake writes the poem in the first person?
Q3. Why might Blake have written this poem?
Q4. Do you think the same kind of problems exist in society today?

Themes — anger, the urban environment...

'A Vision' touches on several similar themes, including anger at the urban landscape and lack of hope for the future. In contrast, 'Hard Water' enthusiastically presents more positive attitudes to it.

Section One — Poems from the Literary Heritage

William Butler Yeats

William Butler Yeats (1865-1939) was born in Dublin. He is often considered to be Ireland's greatest ever poet. As well as poetry, Yeats wrote many plays and won the Nobel Prize for Literature.

The Wild Swans at Coole

The trees are in their autumn beauty,
The woodland paths are dry,
Under the October twilight the water
Mirrors a still sky;
5 Upon the brimming water among the stones
Are nine-and-fifty swans.

The nineteenth autumn has come upon me
Since I first made my count;
I saw, before I had well finished,
10 All suddenly mount
And scatter wheeling in great broken rings
Upon their clamorous wings.

I have looked upon those brilliant creatures,
And now my heart is sore.
15 All's changed since I, hearing at twilight,
The first time on this shore,
The bell-beat of their wings above my head,
Trod with a lighter tread.

Unwearied still, lover by lover,
20 They paddle in the cold
Companionable streams or climb the air;
Their hearts have not grown old;
Passion or conquest, wander where they will,
Attend upon them still.

25 But now they drift on the still water,
Mysterious, beautiful;
Among what rushes will they build,
By what lake's edge or pool
Delight men's eyes when I awake some day
30 To find they have flown away?

Annotations:
- *When he wrote this, Yeats was unmarried and in his early fifties — he might have thought he was in the 'autumn' of his life.*
- *Scene sounds calm and peaceful. Alliteration of soft 's' adds to gentle mood.*
- *Words suggest something growing old or coming to an end — tone is sad and reflective.*
- *Introduces the theme of the passing of time.*
- *Sudden movement of swans marks change in tone.*
- *Words describing action, movement and noise, contrast with earlier stillness — perhaps emphasising power of the swans.*
- *A lot's happened since his last visit — he could be talking about World War One and the Irish Civil War.*
- *Contrast between swans and him — he feels old and tired but the swans still seem young and full of life.*
- *Reminds us of the swans' noise — also gives the impression of church bells and time being rung out.*
- *Suggests that the first time he was here he was younger and full of hope, but now he's feeling tired.*
- *Image of the swans happy and in love. Swans tend to mate for life — perhaps he wishes he could do the same.*
- *More implied contrasts between him and the swans. Despite all the time that's passed the swans don't seem to have aged.*
- *Swans are free to go where they like — maybe he's envious of this.*
- *Admiration for the swans.*
- *Contemplative mood again.*
- *Feeling of loss. Sums up the whole poem — he's drawn to the beauty of the swans, but they also make him sad.*

POEM DICTIONARY
clamorous — noisy
companionable — friendly

Section One — Poems from the Literary Heritage

The Wild Swans at Coole

Yeats is watching some swans on the lake at Coole — a house in Ireland owned by his friend. As he's describing them, we see that they make him think about his life and old age.

You've Got to Know What the Poem's About

1) It's the end of an autumn day and the poet is standing on the shore of the lake at Coole.
2) A group of swans suddenly take off, disturbing the peace, and he thinks about seeing them the last time he was there. A lot's changed since then — but unlike him, the swans don't seem to have aged.
3) The swans seem to represent things he wishes he had — like love and freedom.
4) When the poet thinks of them leaving at the end of the poem, there's a real sense of sadness and loss.

Learn About the Form, Structure and Language

1) FORM — The first person narrator gives a feeling of nostalgia to the poem. It sounds like it could be the poet himself. The ABCBDD rhyme scheme is quite complicated — it's controlled, but not completely rigid.
2) STRUCTURE — At the start of the poem, the tone is calm and gentle, but it becomes livelier when the swans take off. The end of the poem is contemplative, possibly showing the effect the swans have had on his thoughts.
3) LANGUAGE ABOUT TIME — The poet seems to have been thinking a lot about ageing and the passing of time when he wrote this poem — there are lots of references to both.
4) CONTRASTS — The swans appear full of life and youth — while he feels old and tired. They're also described as lovers and companions — something the poet may be envious of.
5) CONTEMPLATIVE LANGUAGE — The language creates a thoughtful and reflective mood — especially in the first and last stanzas.

She may not have looked wild, but Sasha was the life and soul of the party.

Remember the Feelings and Attitudes in the Poem

1) SADNESS — The poet seems sad about the passing of time. The swans seem to remind him of things he wants, but perhaps doesn't have.
2) LOVE OF NATURE — Although the swans make him sad, he clearly loves watching them. The surrounding landscape is also lovingly described.

Go a Step Further and give a Personal Response

Have a go at answering these questions to help you come up with your own ideas about the poem:
Q1. How does the title make you feel about the poem?
Q2. What do you think the overall tone of poem is and how does Yeats create it?
Q3. Yeats was in his fifties when he wrote this poem, but he went on to get married, have children and live another twenty or so years. Does that surprise you? Why / why not?

Themes — memory, reflection, sadness...

The narrator of 'The Blackbird of Glanmore' also thinks about his life in a place that means a lot to him. 'Cold Knap Lake' and 'Crossing the Loch' include the themes of memory and reflection.

Section One — Poems from the Literary Heritage

William Wordsworth

Annotations (right side):
- Complete change in tone. Simple word, but a lot of power. Emphasised by starting the sentence and by the comma (and pause) after it.
- A mountain appears on the horizon. Very different language now — darker and more threatening.
- Starting to sound like a bad dream. Language is more agitated — contrast to earlier confidence.
- Contrasts with the mountain and his earlier self.
- The event has had a big impact on him — 'grave' means serious, but may also be a reminder of his own mortality.
- The narrator is left feeling alone and afraid.
- The narrator no longer thinks of nature in terms of these pretty images — he's learnt there's more to it than that.
- Unsettling image — helps us to empathise with him. Huge contrast to the tone and mood at start.

Annotations (left side):
- The mountain is personified. Ugly image — contrast to earlier beautiful images of the boat ('elfin', 'swan').
- The mountain is calm, powerful and in control — contrasts with the narrator's new-found fear.
- He's now afraid and wants to hide away — he feels like an intruder.
- The impact was long lasting.
- He seems in awe of nature's power.
- Suggests that he thinks the mountains are alive, but he's not sure how.

Poem:

When, from behind that craggy steep till then
The horizon's bound, a huge peak, black and huge,
As if with voluntary power instinct,
Upreared its head. I struck and struck again,
25 And growing still in stature the grim shape
Towered up between me and the stars, and still,
For so it seemed, with purpose of its own
And measured motion like a living thing,
Strode after me. With trembling oars I turned,
30 And through the silent water stole my way
Back to the covert of the willow tree;
There in her mooring-place I left my bark, —
And through the meadows homeward went, in grave
And serious mood; but after I had seen
35 That spectacle, for many days, my brain
Worked with a dim and undetermined sense
Of unknown modes of being; o'er my thoughts
There hung a darkness, call it solitude
Or blank desertion. No familiar shapes
40 Remained, no pleasant images of trees,
Of sea or sky, no colours of green fields;
But huge and mighty forms, that do not live
Like living men, moved slowly through the mind
By day, and were a trouble to my dreams.

POEM DICTIONARY
stealth — secrecy
pinnace — an old kind of sail boat
lustily — enthusiastically
covert — shelter
bark — a small boat

Section One — Poems from the Literary Heritage

William Wordsworth

William Wordsworth (1770-1850) was one of England's greatest poets. He was born in Cockermouth, and wrote many poems about the Lake District.

Extract from **The Prelude**

One summer evening (led by her) I found
A little boat tied to a willow tree
Within a rocky cave, its usual home.
Straight I unloosed her chain, and stepping in
5   Pushed from the shore. It was an act of stealth
And troubled pleasure, nor without the voice
Of mountain-echoes did my boat move on;
Leaving behind her still, on either side,
Small circles glittering idly in the moon,
10 Until they melted all into one track
Of sparkling light. But now, like one who rows,
Proud of his skill, to reach a chosen point
With an unswerving line, I fixed my view
Upon the summit of a craggy ridge,
15 The horizon's utmost boundary; far above
Was nothing but the stars and the grey sky.
She was an elfin pinnace; lustily
I dipped my oars into the silent lake,
And, as I rose upon the stroke, my boat
20 Went heaving through the water like a swan;

Annotations:
- Happy, rural image.
- Narrator appears confident.
- Pretty images reassure you again — narrator seems happy.
- Again, narrator seems confident, maybe a bit arrogant. This contrasts with later in the poem.
- 'A fairy boat' — scene is magical and otherworldly, but still not threatening.
- Unclear here who 'her' is. Could be the boat — an earlier part of the poem suggests it's nature, personified.
- Seems familiar to him.
- Clues that something isn't quite right.
- Could be pretty or menacing.
- Sounds like he's still enjoying himself here.
- Could be a peaceful or a menacing image.
- Again, he seems confident and in control — enhances the contrast with the next line.

Section One — Poems from the Literary Heritage

THIS IS A FLAP.
FOLD THIS PAGE OUT.

The Prelude

This is an extract from a much longer poem called The Prelude (it's made up of fourteen different books). Wordsworth worked on the poem for over fifty years. At least he had a fair bit to show for it.

You've Got to Know What the Poem's About

1) It's a summer evening and the narrator finds a boat tied up to a willow tree.
2) He unties the boat and takes it out on the lake.
3) The narrator seems happy and confident. He describes a beautiful, peaceful scene — but there are already clues that things may be about to go wrong.
4) A mountain appears on the horizon and the scene changes. The narrator becomes afraid of the size and power of the mountain.
5) He turns the boat around and goes home, but his encounter has troubled him. His view of nature has changed.

The mountain scared Bill, but he wasn't sure why.

Learn About the Form, Structure and Language

1) **FORM** — This extract is written in first person narrative. It sounds personal — perhaps it's describing a turning point in the poet's life. The use of blank verse makes it sound serious and important. The rhythm is a regular iambic pentameter, which makes it sound like natural speech.
2) **STRUCTURE** — In the first half of the extract the tone is fairly light and carefree. There's a distinct change when the mountain appears though — it becomes darker and much more fearful.
3) **CONFIDENT LANGUAGE** — The narrator appears sure of himself at first — almost arrogant in his view of himself and his place in the world. He gives the impression of feeling powerful.
4) **DRAMATIC LANGUAGE** — You see glimpses of threatening language at the beginning of the extract, but it becomes much more intense after the arrival of the mountain. Nature takes on the power the narrator thought he once had.
5) **FEARFUL LANGUAGE** — The narrator is far less confident at the end of the story. He's been changed by his encounter.
6) **BEAUTIFUL LANGUAGE** — The poet begins by creating a series of pretty, pastoral images of nature. The whole experience seems magical to start with and the narrator is happy and content.

Remember the Feelings and Attitudes in the Poem

1) **CONFIDENCE** — The narrator feels comfortable and in control to start with, but his confidence in himself and the world around him is shaken by this one event.
2) **FEAR** — Nature is shown to be powerful — more powerful than a human being. The narrator is left with a feeling of awe and respect for this, but he's also scared by it.

Go a Step Further and give a Personal Response

Have a go at answering these questions to help you come up with your own ideas about the poem:
Q1. How do the narrator's feelings change over the course of the poem? What causes these changes?
Q2. Can you empathise with the narrator? Is his reaction understandable?
Q3. What impression of nature do you have by the end of the poem?

Themes — the power of nature, life-changing events...

Nature is presented as being very powerful in several poems, including 'The Moment' and 'Below the Green Corrie'. The latter is also about an encounter with a mountain that changes the narrator's life.

Section One — Poems from the Literary Heritage

Emily Brontë

Emily Brontë (1818-1848) was born in Yorkshire, the second eldest of the three Brontë sisters. After studying for a time in Brussels, the sisters published a collection of their poetry under pseudonyms (Emily's being 'Ellis Bell') to avoid discrimination against female writers.

Spellbound

The night is darkening round me,
The wild winds coldly blow;
But a tyrant spell has bound me
And I cannot, cannot go.

5 The giant trees are bending
Their bare boughs weighed with snow.
And the storm is fast descending,
And yet I cannot go.

Clouds beyond clouds above me,
10 Wastes beyond wastes below;
But nothing drear can move me;
I will not, cannot go.

Annotations:
- Sounds magical, but we don't know if it's a good or a bad thing.
- Suggests the spell is forceful and unreasonable.
- Another image of the storm's force.
- Sounds irrational — something's stopping her.
- Could be trying to create an image of heaven and hell — emphasises mystic feeling of poem.
- A subtle change from before — suggests that it's maybe her choice to stay after all.
- Sets a dramatic scene which builds up through poem.
- Shows the power of the storm — frightening, but maybe exciting too.
- Repetition emphasises the power of the spell. She's desperate to get somewhere safe, but can't.
- Images of the storm's power. Alliteration sounds almost chant-like.
- The narrator repeats the word 'me' a lot. Perhaps it's so she doesn't feel lost in the storm — or to make it sound like nature's casting the spell directly on her.
- Sounds dark and foreboding. Builds up the idea she's in danger.

POEM DICTIONARY
tyrant — a cruel ruler or dictator
drear — dreary, gloomy

Section One — Poems from the Literary Heritage

Spellbound

The narrator is caught out in a <u>storm</u> and claims she <u>can't leave</u> — never mind the <u>snow</u> and <u>gale force winds</u>. Silly girl. She'll catch her death, as my grandma would say.

You've Got to Know What the Poem's About

1) Night is falling and the narrator is caught in the beginnings of a <u>storm</u>.
2) Even though the storm is getting <u>worse</u> and she knows she should go, the narrator says she's bound by a <u>spell</u> and <u>can't leave</u>.
3) The <u>power</u> of the storm seems to be both <u>frightening</u> and <u>appealing</u>. The narrator finishes by saying that she doesn't <u>want</u> to leave.

Belinda was spellbound by nature from a young age.

Learn About the Form, Structure and Language

1) <u>FORM</u> — The regular <u>four line</u> stanzas make the poem look like a <u>song</u> or a <u>spell</u>. The regular <u>iambic</u> rhythm and <u>ABAB</u> rhyme scheme make the poem <u>sound</u> chant- or spell-like too.
2) <u>STRUCTURE</u> — All the way through the poem, we're made to feel like the narrator is under the <u>complete control</u> of the spell. But on the <u>last line</u>, we discover that she might also be acting of her own <u>free will</u>.
3) <u>DRAMATIC LANGUAGE</u> — The <u>force</u> of the storm and the <u>power</u> of nature come across in the language the poet uses to describe them.
4) <u>REPETITION</u> — Again this makes the poem sound like a <u>chant</u> — it also emphasises the feeling that the narrator has been <u>entranced</u> by nature.

Remember the Feelings and Attitudes in the Poem

1) <u>ENCHANTMENT</u> — As the title suggests, the narrator feels like she's under the influence of a <u>spell</u>. The whole poem appears to be <u>written</u> like a spell too.
2) <u>CONFLICT</u> — The narrator seems <u>confused</u> by the storm. Logic tells her it's <u>dangerous</u> and she should <u>leave</u>, but its sense of magic makes her want to <u>stay</u>.

Go a Step Further and give a Personal Response

Have a go at <u>answering</u> these <u>questions</u> to help you come up with <u>your own ideas</u> about the poem:
- Q1. What is your first impression of the poem from the title?
- Q2. How do you think the narrator feels about nature?
- Q3. Do you think her feelings change during the poem?
- Q4. Can you empathise with how the narrator feels?

Themes — the magic of nature, intense feelings...

'Crossing the Loch' is about the magic and mystery of an encounter with nature.
'Storm in the Black Forest' describes a storm passionately, as if under its influence or spell.

Section One — Poems from the Literary Heritage

Norman MacCaig

Norman MacCaig (1910-1996) was a Scottish poet born in Edinburgh. He started out as a primary school teacher, later working for the University of Stirling in Scotland and publishing several works of poetry. He won the Queen's Gold Medal for Poetry in 1985.

Below the Green Corrie

The mountains gathered round me
like bandits. Their leader
swaggered up close in the dark light,
full of threats, full of thunders.

5 But it was they who stood and delivered.
They gave me their money and their lives.
They filled me with mountains and thunders.

My life was enriched
with an infusion of theirs.
10 I clambered downhill through the ugly weather.
And when I turned to look goodbye
to those marvellous prowlers
a sunshaft had pierced the clouds
and their leader,
15 that swashbuckling mountain,
was wearing
a bandolier of light.

Annotations:
- Sounds like something from a film — scary, but fun.
- The mountains seem bold and full of life.
- Unclear as to whether they chose to or he made them.
- Repetition emphasises that the mountains have given him the things that make them great and powerful.
- Makes him seem human and ordinary — contrasts with the mountains.
- In awe of mountains.
- Beautiful, magical image. Adds to the feeling that the mountains are special.
- Personification of mountains — attention-grabbing image.
- Threatening — but sounds a bit exaggerated. Maybe the mountains are bluffing.
- Clichés from films suggest the mountains have the ability to be life threatening, but are also places of fun and enjoyment.
- More serious now — and grateful for what the mountains gave him. They've become a part of him and his life.
- Creates feeling of respect for the mountains — he communicates with them like they're real people.
- Sounds wild, but heroic. Affectionate tone.
- Strong image — can imagine the mountain shooting light.

POEM DICTIONARY
corrie — a hollow on a mountainside
swashbuckling — wild, adventurous
bandolier — an over-the-shoulder belt that normally holds gun cartridges

Section One — Poems from the Literary Heritage

Below the Green Corrie

In this poem, the narrator has a weirdly exciting experience with some mountains. Happy days...

You've Got to Know What the Poem's About

1) The narrator is out walking in the mountains.
2) At first the mountains seem threatening — they gather round him like bandits.
3) But instead of carrying out their threats, they give their power to him.
4) As he climbs back down the mountains, the narrator feels enriched by the experience.
5) We're left with the impression that the mountains are wild and heroic.

Learn About the Form, Structure and Language

1) **FORM** — The poem is written in free verse — there's no rhyme or regular rhythm. This makes the thoughts and feelings of the first person narrator sound more natural — as does the use of enjambment.
2) **STRUCTURE** — The stanzas all have very distinct ideas. The first sounds a bit threatening, while the second surprises us by turning the tables on the mountains. The third stanza is more thoughtful and covers the after-effects of the incident.
3) **BANDIT IMAGERY** — The image of the mountains as bandits is humorous. We see the mountains as wild and threatening — but fun and exciting at the same time.
4) **RESPECTFUL LANGUAGE** — Although the tone of the poem seems light-hearted in places, the narrator respects the mountains' power. He knows that they're capable of terrible things, but also that they have a lot to offer.
5) **VISUAL LANGUAGE** — A lot of the images in this poem are very vivid. They really help us to picture the scene. The final line especially is very memorable, leaving us with a lasting impression of the mountains' greatness.

Remember the Feelings and Attitudes in the Poem

1) **RESPECT FOR NATURE** — The mountains in this poem have the power to harm the narrator, but they also have the power to enrich his life. As bandits, they're portrayed as exciting and thrilling — if there wasn't an element of danger to them, this might not be the case.
2) **ENJOYMENT** — The narrator feels he has gained a lot by experiencing the mountains. They seem to have changed him as a person.

Go a Step Further and give a Personal Response

Have a go at answering these questions to help you come up with your own ideas about the poem:
Q1. What did you expect the poem to be like from the title? Were you right?
Q2. Do you think the images of bandits and highwaymen used to describe the mountains are effective?
Q3. Why do you think the poet chooses to finish on the image that he does?

Themes — awe of nature, life-changing events...

'The Prelude' is about a life-changing event that leaves the narrator in awe of a mountain — but his experience of nature is not a positive one. 'The Moment' also talks about the power of nature.

Section One — Poems from the Literary Heritage

D H Lawrence

David Herbert Lawrence (1885-1930) was born in a mining town in Nottinghamshire, before moving to London to start a career in teaching. Following an illness in 1911, he left his job to become a full-time writer and later travelled the world extensively.

Storm in the Black Forest

Now it is almost night, from the bronzey soft sky
jugfull after jugfull of pure white liquid fire, bright white
tipples over and spills down,
and is gone
5   and gold-bronze flutters bent through the thick upper air.

And as the electric liquid pours out, sometimes
a still brighter white snake wriggles among it, spilled
and tumbling wriggling down the sky:
and then the heavens cackle with uncouth sounds.

10   And the rain won't come, the rain refuses to come!

This is the electricity that man is supposed to have mastered
chained, subjugated to his use!
supposed to!

POEM DICTIONARY
uncouth — rude
subjugated — brought under control

Section One — Poems from the Literary Heritage

Storm in the Black Forest

This is another poem about a storm. You'll be delighted to find one on the next page too. Now I know we're a nation famed for talking about our weather, but this is bordering on the ridiculous...

You've Got to Know What the Poem's About

1) The narrator describes the beginnings of a lightning storm.
2) The storm builds in power and intensity, but it still doesn't rain. The rain seems to have a mind of its own.
3) The narrator ends by questioning humans' power — having seen the storm, he doesn't believe that mankind can ever hope to control nature.

Emily had no control over the electricity in her hair.

Learn About the Form, Structure and Language

1) FORM — The poem is written in free verse and the lines are irregular in length. It makes the poem sound natural and a bit chaotic, like a storm — as does the use of enjambment. Exclamation marks in the final stanza add to the excitement that's built up with the storm.
2) STRUCTURE — The poet doesn't make his point until the last stanza. It seems sudden and direct after the vivid descriptions of nature before it.
3) VISUAL IMAGERY — The vivid language helps us to picture the beauty and power of the storm. It makes it seem real and exciting.
4) REPETITION — Repetition of words and phrases makes the narrator sound entranced. It also makes his descriptions sound spontaneous — as if he's describing events as he sees them.
5) SCORNFUL LANGUAGE — The final lines of the poem are critical and mocking. Humans' belief that they can control nature is made to seem arrogant and foolish.

Remember the Feelings and Attitudes in the Poem

1) AWE — The storm is described as beautiful and powerful, with a mind of its own.
2) SCEPTICISM — Humans think they can control the world around them — but we have no control over the electricity in the storm. Nature is wild and untameable, whatever we believe.

Go a Step Further and give a Personal Response

Have a go at answering these questions to help you come up with your own ideas about the poem:

Q1. Is the language used to describe the storm effective? What effect does it have on you?
Q2. Why do you think so many of the poet's descriptions involve colour?
Q3. How does the tone of the poem change in the last stanza?
Q4. What do you think the poet's referring to when he talks about subjugating nature?

Themes — the power of nature, intense feelings...

'Spellbound' is also about someone captivated by a powerful storm. The narrator of 'Wind' is stuck in the middle of a storm too, but he appears afraid rather than enchanted by its strength.

Section One — Poems from the Literary Heritage

Ted Hughes

Ted Hughes (1930-1998) served as the British Poet Laureate from 1984 until he died. Born in West Yorkshire, he studied at Pembroke College, Cambridge, later spending most of his life in Devon.

Wind

This house has been far out at sea all night,
The woods crashing through darkness, the booming hills,
Winds stampeding the fields under the window
Floundering black astride and blinding wet

5   Till day rose; then under an orange sky
The hills had new places, and wind wielded
Blade-light, luminous black and emerald,
Flexing like the lens of a mad eye.

At noon I scaled along the house-side as far as
10 The coal-house door. Once I looked up -
Through the brunt wind that dented the balls of my eyes
The tent of the hills drummed and strained its guyrope,

The fields quivering, the skyline a grimace,
At any second to bang and vanish with a flap;
15 The wind flung a magpie away and a black-
Back gull bent like an iron bar slowly. The house

Rang like some fine green goblet in the note
That any second would shatter it. Now deep
In chairs, in front of the great fire, we grip
20 Our hearts and cannot entertain book, thought,

Or each other. We watch the fire blazing,
And feel the roots of the house move, but sit on,
Seeing the window tremble to come in,
Hearing the stones cry out under the horizons.

POEM DICTIONARY
wielded — brandished a weapon
luminous — glowing
brunt — main force
guyrope — rope securing a tent to the ground

Section One — Poems from the Literary Heritage

Wind

This poem is a <u>dramatic account</u> of a <u>storm</u> and its <u>power</u>. This could be a real storm, or it could be a <u>metaphor</u> for an <u>argument</u> or series of arguments which threatened to <u>destroy a relationship</u>.

You've Got to Know What the Poem's About

1) There's been a <u>violent storm</u> overnight.
2) The <u>wind</u> is still <u>strong</u> the next morning when the narrator goes out to inspect the <u>damage</u>.
3) The storm continues to batter the <u>house</u> and surrounding landscape.
4) There's nothing the people in the house can do except <u>sit and wait</u> for it to end. They're <u>scared</u> of the <u>harm</u> it will cause.

Learn About the Form, Structure and Language

1) <u>FORM</u> — This a <u>personal</u> experience — it's written in the <u>first person</u> so we can <u>empathise</u> with the feelings of the narrator. The use of <u>enjambment</u> makes the poem <u>sound</u> stormy and <u>uncontrolled</u>.
2) <u>STRUCTURE</u> — The first five stanzas describe different aspects of the storm, but the last two stanzas are about the <u>people in the house</u> — the poem concludes with the storm's <u>effects</u> on them.
3) <u>METAPHOR and SIMILE</u> — Hughes has used some extremely <u>effective</u> metaphors to help us visualise the <u>destructive force</u> and power of the storm. It's also possible that the whole poem is a metaphor for a <u>stormy relationship</u>.
4) <u>PERSONIFICATION</u> — The poet has made the <u>normally invisible</u> wind sound like a <u>real, solid being</u> — this makes it sound <u>stronger</u> and more <u>frightening</u>. The idea that the wind is <u>deliberate</u> in its actions makes it more unnerving.
5) <u>DRAMATIC LANGUAGE</u> — The poet is writing about a <u>dramatic subject</u> — he uses <u>powerful</u>, often <u>violent</u> language to reflect this.

Jack's wind was threatening to destroy his relationship with Lisa.

Remember the Feelings and Attitudes in the Poem

1) <u>THREAT</u> — The <u>wind</u> in this poem is capable of <u>destroying everything</u> in its path. If the storm is a <u>metaphor</u> for an <u>argument</u>, then that argument also has the power to destroy.
2) <u>FEAR</u> — The couple in this poem are <u>afraid</u> of the storm and what it is <u>capable of doing</u>. All they can do is <u>hide away</u> and <u>wait</u> for it to be over.

Go a Step Further and give a Personal Response

Have a go at <u>answering</u> these <u>questions</u> to help you come up with <u>your own ideas</u> about the poem:

Q1. Choose one of the images that Hughes uses to describe the storm. What impression does it give of the storm?
Q2. Why do you think the poet has chosen to personify the wind in places?
Q3. Do you think the poem is about a storm or an argument? Are there other possible meanings?

Themes — the power of nature, lack of hope...

The poems 'Spellbound' and 'Storm in the Black Forest' are also about very powerful storms. The poems 'London' and 'A Vision' have a similar absence of hope for the future in their final stanzas.

Section One — Poems from the Literary Heritage

Seamus Heaney

Seamus Heaney was born in 1939 in County Derry, Northern Ireland. He grew up on his father's farm before going to university in Belfast. His younger brother Christopher died in a road accident aged four.

The Blackbird of Glanmore

On the grass when I arrive,
Filling the stillness with life,
But ready to scare off
At the very first wrong move.
5   In the ivy when I leave.

It's you, blackbird, I love.

I park, pause, take heed.
Breathe. Just breathe and sit
And lines I once translated
10   Come back: 'I want away
To the house of death, to my father

Under the low clay roof.'

And I think of one gone to him,
A little stillness dancer –
15   Haunter-son, lost brother –
Cavorting through the yard,
So glad to see me home,

My homesick first term over.

And think of a neighbour's words
20   Long after the accident:
'Yon bird on the shed roof,
Up on the ridge for weeks –
I said nothing at the time

But I never liked yon bird.'

25   The automatic lock
Clunks shut, the blackbird's panic
Is shortlived, for a second
I've a bird's eye view of myself,
A shadow on raked gravel

30   In front of my house of life.

Hedge-hop, I am absolute
For you, your ready talkback,
Your each stand-offish comeback,
Your picky, nervy goldbeak –
35   On the grass when I arrive,

In the ivy when I leave.

POEM DICTIONARY
take heed — pay attention
cavorting — bouncing around
yon — that

The Blackbird of Glanmore

Heaney arrives home from his first term at university to find a blackbird on the grass outside. The sight of the bird makes him happy and he watches it for a while. As he does so he thinks about his brother's death.

You've Got to Know What the Poem's About

1) The poet is watching a blackbird on the grass. He seems pleased to see it there.
2) As he watches the bird, he remembers part of a poem that makes him think of his brother's death.
3) He also remembers his neighbour's comments after his brother's accident — that a blackbird seen sitting on the shed roof in previous weeks had been a sign that death was coming.
4) He considers his own mortality as the bird takes fright at the sound of the car's lock.
5) The bird soon returns and the poem goes back to the beginning.

Learn About the Form, Structure and Language

1) FORM — The poem has an irregular rhythm, created through features like caesura and enjambment. There's no rhyme scheme either. These features make the poem sound more natural — as if you're really hearing the speaker's thoughts.
2) STRUCTURE — The poem is circular — the tone is happy and light in the first and last stanzas, but more reflective in the middle four. The pace changes to match this. Lines at the beginning of the poem are also repeated again at the end.
3) CONTRASTS — There are lots of references to life and death. The blackbird in particular is linked to both these things.
4) CONTEMPLATIVE LANGUAGE — There's a feeling of sadness and loss in places — especially when the speaker thinks of the past or future.
5) JOYFUL LANGUAGE — The words chosen to describe the blackbird are designed to mimic the bird's bright, lively movements. They also give a sense of the happiness Heaney feels at seeing the bird.

'What are you looking at?'

Remember the Feelings and Attitudes in the Poem

1) LOVE — There are two loves here, one happy, one sad. Love for the blackbird makes the speaker happy, but it also makes him remember a love for his brother that makes him sad.
2) LOSS — Most of the poem is about the loss of Heaney's brother in an accident. The poet also thinks about loss when he contemplates his own death — leaving nothing but a shadow.

Go a Step Further and give a Personal Response

Have a go at answering these questions to help you come up with your own ideas about the poem:

Q1. Why do you think Heaney repeats the phrases "On the grass when I arrive" and "In the ivy when I leave" near the start and at the end of the poem?
Q2. What do you think the mood of the poem is? How is this mood created?
Q3. Do you think Heaney agrees at all with the neighbour's point of view that the bird was an omen?
Q4. How does the poem make you feel about death and how does Heaney create this effect?

Themes — memory, sadness, relationships...

In 'The Wild Swans at Coole', a group of swans cause the narrator to reflect sadly on his life.
In 'Price We Pay for the Sun' the narrator talks about her family and the place she grew up.

Section Two — Contemporary Poems

Simon Armitage

Simon Armitage was born in 1963 in West Yorkshire. As well as poetry, he's also written four stage plays, and writes for TV, film and radio.

A Vision

The future was a beautiful place, once.
Remember the full-blown balsa-wood town
on public display in the Civic Hall?
The ring-bound sketches, artists' impressions,
5   blueprints of smoked glass and tubular steel,
board-game suburbs, modes of transportation
like fairground rides or executive toys.
Cities like *dreams*, cantilevered by light.

And people like us at the bottle-bank
10 next to the cycle-path, or dog-walking
over tended strips of fuzzy-felt grass,
or model drivers, motoring home in

electric cars. Or after the late show –
strolling the boulevard. They were the plans,
15 all underwritten in the neat left-hand
of architects – a true, legible script.

I pulled that future out of the north wind
at the landfill site, stamped with today's date,
riding the air with other such futures,
20 all unlived in and now fully extinct.

POEM DICTIONARY
balsa wood — lightweight wood used for model making
cantilevered — supported
boulevard — a wide, open street
underwritten — guaranteed
legible — neat, easily read

Section Two — Contemporary Poems

A Vision

A poem about <u>town planning</u> — ah, joy. If only there were more. It's a subject <u>shamefully ignored</u> by most poets if you ask me — a bit like <u>lawn-mowing</u> and <u>accountancy</u>. I honestly can't think why.

You've Got to Know What the Poem's About

1) The poet <u>remembers</u> what old visions for the <u>future</u> were like.
2) He talks about how the <u>ideal future town</u> was supposed to look — and what was supposed to happen there. He gives the impression that the plans for this town were <u>unrealistic</u> — and that the vision of a perfect world was always going to be <u>impossible</u> to achieve.
3) He eventually finds the plans in the <u>dump</u> — dreams of the future contrast starkly with the bleak <u>realities</u> of the present. Things <u>did not</u> turn out the way people <u>hoped</u>.

Learn About the Form, Structure and Language

1) <u>FORM</u> — The poem is narrated in the <u>first person</u>. The tidy <u>ten-syllable</u> lines look <u>neat</u> and <u>controlled</u> on the page — possibly echoing the manufactured drawings and designs in the old future plans.
2) <u>STRUCTURE</u> — The narrator begins by <u>reminiscing</u> about the <u>future plans</u>. He seems to <u>dismiss</u> these dreams as <u>pointless</u> from the very first line. In the final lines we discover that they <u>never came true</u>.
3) <u>IMAGERY</u> — A lot of the images in the poem are used to create the feeling that the plans for the future were either <u>unrealistic</u> and <u>fake</u>, or <u>vague</u> with no real <u>substance</u>.
4) <u>CONTRASTS</u> — The main contrast in the poem is the difference between the <u>dream</u> of an <u>ideal future</u> and the harsh <u>reality</u> of the present. This adds to the <u>ironic</u> tone of the poem.
5) <u>LANGUAGE ABOUT THE FUTURE</u> — This language is <u>hopeful</u> — it shows what an <u>ideal</u> future would be like.

The girls were a vision in florals and white LYCRA®.

Remember the Feelings and Attitudes in the Poem

1) <u>IDEALISM vs REALITY</u> — There's a stark <u>contrast</u> between dreams and reality. The poem suggests the plans were too out of touch with the lives of <u>real people</u>.
2) <u>CYNICISM</u> — The poet appears cynical about the idea of planning the <u>perfect</u> town. He appears to suggest that the dream could <u>never</u> have come true.

Go a Step Further and give a Personal Response

Have a go at <u>answering</u> these <u>questions</u> to help you come up with <u>your own ideas</u> about the poem:
Q1. How do you think Armitage's narrator feels about the old vision of the future?
Q2. Why did this vision fail, according to the poem?
Q3. Do you think that all visions of the future are unrealistic?
Q4. Do you think the poet is saying that it's silly to be hopeful about the future? Do you agree?

Themes — anger, sadness, the urban environment...
The poem 'London' also looks angrily at a bleak urban environment and offers no hope for its future improvement. This lack of hope contrasts with the optimistic ending of 'Neighbours'.

Section Two — Contemporary Poems

Margaret Atwood

Margaret Atwood was born in 1939 in Canada. She graduated in 1961 from the University of Toronto, and has since taught at various Canadian universities as well as writing professionally, receiving numerous awards for both her poetry and works of fiction.

The Moment

The moment when, after many years
of hard work and a long voyage
you stand in the centre of your room,
house, half-acre, square mile, island, country,
5 knowing at last how you got there,
and say, *I own this*,

is the same moment when the trees unloose
their soft arms from around you,
the birds take back their language,
10 the cliffs fissure and collapse,
the air moves back from you like a wave
and you can't breathe.

No, they whisper. *You own nothing.
You were a visitor, time after time
15 climbing the hill, planting the flag, proclaiming.
We never belonged to you.
You never found us.
It was always the other way round.*

Annotations:
- Use of 'the' sounds definite — implies that what the poet describes will happen to us all.
- It's not clear who the narrator is addressing here, but it seems to be a person who feels their life is complete.
- Another egocentric phrase — even slightly arrogant.
- Nature doesn't need to shout — powerful, but more subtle than the arrogant human.
- Very certain, definite language — nature is clearly boss.
- Sounds egocentric — something that nature appears to object to later.
- Becoming clearer that she could be addressing any one of us — listing different types of life.
- Unsettling language.
- Stanza becomes more violent and frightening as the language becomes more dramatic.
- Very definite — humans have nothing. Nature's in charge.
- Again, the human is arrogant, egocentric.

POEM DICTIONARY
voyage — long journey
fissure — split
proclaiming — announcing

Section Two — Contemporary Poems

The Moment

This is a poem about humans thinking they're in charge of the world around them — but really nature is the one in control. And, um, that's about it really. Excellent.

You've Got to Know What the Poem's About

1) In the first stanza, the narrator seems to be talking to someone who feels their life is sorted — they've achieved their goals, they know (or think they know) what life is about.
2) But it quickly becomes clear that they've got it wrong. At the moment they think their life is exactly how they want it, nature arrives and starts to take everything back — even the air we need to breathe.
3) The last stanza makes it clear that we don't own anything — nature is in control of us.

Learn About the Form, Structure and Language

1) FORM — There's no rhyme scheme, which makes the poem sound natural and matter of fact. The first two stanzas are all one sentence — with a big shift in thinking from start to finish. It's a lot to take in and it helps to build up the drama and intensity of the poem.
2) STRUCTURE — The order of ideas in this poem is very important. It emphasises the contrast between the way we see things (first stanza) and the way they really are (last stanza). Pauses in between the stanzas emphasise the difference in tone.
3) ARROGANCE — Humans come across as being self-centred and proud. They might believe they're in control — but it's nature that has the real power.
4) DRAMATIC LANGUAGE — This shows the power of nature over human beings. It also adds to the fear and shock you feel reading the second stanza after the calmness of the first stanza.
5) CERTAINTY — The language creates a very definite tone — it says nature is in charge.

Remember the Feelings and Attitudes in the Poem

1) POWER OF NATURE — Nature has the power to do terrible things — and to take away everything people own. There's a contrast between bold, boastful people and quiet, confident nature.
2) HUMAN FAILINGS — People's belief that they own everything and are in control of the world around them is made to seem foolish.

Ahh. Nice nature.

Go a Step Further and give a Personal Response

Have a go at answering these questions to help you come up with your own ideas about the poem:
Q1. Do you think the first stanza is an effective beginning for the poem? Why / why not?
Q2. What impression do you get of nature from stanzas two and three? How is this impression created?
Q3. What do you think the title means? Why do you think Atwood chose this title?
Q4. Do you think Atwood's message is aimed at anyone in particular?

Themes — the power of nature...

Many poems are about the power of nature over mankind, for example 'Wind' and 'Storm in the Black Forest'. 'The Prelude' is about man's loss of certainty on encountering the power of nature.

Section Two — Contemporary Poems

Gillian Clarke

Gillian Clarke was born in 1937 in Cardiff. She teaches creative writing at the University of Glamorgan. Many of her poems reflect her cultural identity and family relationships in Wales.

Cold Knap Lake

We once watched a crowd
pull a drowned child from the lake.
Blue-lipped and dressed in water's long green silk
she lay for dead.

5 Then kneeling on the earth,
a heroine, her red head bowed,
her wartime cotton frock soaked,
my mother gave a stranger's child her breath.
The crowd stood silent,
10 drawn by the dread of it.

The child breathed, bleating
and rosy in my mother's hands.
My father took her home to a poor house
and watched her thrashed for almost drowning.

15 Was I there?
Or is that troubled surface something else
shadowy under the dipped fingers of willows
where satiny mud blooms in cloudiness
after the treading, heavy webs of swans
20 as their wings beat and whistle on the air?

All lost things lie under closing water
in that lake with the poor man's daughter.

Sounds like she's dead at this point.

The girl's covered in pond weeds. The "silk" contrasts with her "poor house" (line 13).

Dramatic descriptions of her mother's bravery.

Her mother's actions while giving mouth-to-mouth make it sound like she's praying.

A selfless act — she clearly admires her mother for it.

Alliteration adds to the drama of the story.

Transformation, from death to life — as if the poet's mother has performed a miracle.

Short line creates a change of tone — she suddenly sounds uncertain.

A shocking image, but it sounds unemotional.

What she saw was dark and vague — her imagination might have created the story from her uncertain memory.

The surface of the lake — but also her uncertain memory.

The water was muddy and unclear, like the memory.

These lines bring together the points she's been discussing, and answer the questions she's been asking herself.

Rhyming couplet brings the poem to a neat conclusion.

POEM DICTIONARY
satiny — smooth, glossy (like satin)

Section Two — Contemporary Poems

Cold Knap Lake

The narrator describes a time when her mother saved a girl who nearly drowned. Then she wonders whether the memory is real or not. Place your bets...

You've Got to Know What the Poem's About

1) The narrator remembers seeing a crowd gathered around a girl who's just been pulled out of a lake.
2) She describes how her mother saved the girl by giving her mouth-to-mouth resuscitation.
3) The narrator's father took the girl home, where she was beaten by her own father.
4) The narrator wonders whether the memory is real. She says memories often become confused.

Learn About the Form, Structure and Language

1) FORM — The first person narrator appears to be the poet herself. The sentences in the poem are long and the poet uses enjambment — the last stanza has only one sentence. This makes the poem sound like someone's thoughts. A rhyming couplet summarises her message.
2) STRUCTURE — The poem begins with confident and detailed descriptions then changes to feelings of confusion and uncertainty in the last stanza. This seems to represent the way we look back on past events and try to make sense of them.
3) DRAMATIC LANGUAGE — The poet's descriptions of how her mother revived the girl make the story sound almost too amazing to be true. This might be why the poet wonders if she's imagined it.
4) PHILOSOPHICAL LANGUAGE — The poet questions herself and wonders about how memories work. The uncertain language in the last two verses adds to the idea that things might not have actually happened as she remembers them. She tries to come up with some answers to tie things together.

Remember the Feelings and Attitudes in the Poem

1) ADMIRATION — The poet admires her mother for saving the girl.
2) CONFUSION — She can't be sure what's real and what's imagined.
3) WONDER — She's fairly philosophical at the end of the poem — she says that memories can get blurred, and that's just how it is.

Real or imaginary?

Go a Step Further and give a Personal Response

Have a go at answering these questions to help you come up with your own ideas about the poem:

Q1. How does Clarke use language to create the feeling of uncertainty in the last two stanzas?
Q2. What do you think the poem suggests about the nature of memories?
Q3. Do you think the incident was real? Does it matter?

Themes — memory, uncertainty...

'Crossing the Loch' is also a poem about the memory of a long-ago event, parts of which are uncertain. The narrator of 'The Prelude' loses his certainty about life during the course of the poem.

Section Two — Contemporary Poems

Grace Nichols

Grace Nichols was born in Guyana in 1950. She was a teacher and journalist in the Caribbean until she moved to Britain in 1977. Both of these cultures, and how they interlink, are important to her.

Price We Pay for the Sun

These islands
not picture postcards
for unravelling tourist
you know
5   these islands real
more real
than flesh and blood
past stone
past foam
10 these islands split
bone

my mother's breasts
like sleeping volcanoes
who know
15 what kinda sulph-furious
cancer tricking her
below
while the wind
constantly whipping
20 my father's tears
to salty hurricanes
and my grandmother's croon
sifting sand
water mirroring palm

25 Poverty is the price
we pay for the sun girl
run come

Annotations:
- Direct — challenges your point of view. Sounds a bit indignant.
- Caribbean dialect — non-standard English.
- Suggests the islands have a deep history — past what you can see today. Maybe even older than stone.
- Emphasises that the islands are a real place, where real people live — not just somewhere to go on holiday.
- Suggests that the islands are hard to live on.
- Links the poet's mum and the islands' landscape — both great in her eyes. Also links her cancer to volcanoes — tragedy waiting and then exploding.
- Suggests her mum might have cancer.
- Word play with 'sulphurous' — links cancer and the volcanoes. Both have the power to destroy.
- Linking the islands to more people who are important to her makes the poem personal.
- More images of destruction on the islands — relentless weather.
- Calm images — show the islands can be peaceful like the tourists believe.
- Suggests the islands are part of the poet's history.
- Might refer to the poet's conflict — the islands are important to her, but they cause pain. She doesn't know whether to stay or go.
- Sudden, unexpected message — the sun keeps the islanders poor.

POEM DICTIONARY
croon — sing softly / soothingly

Price We Pay for the Sun

The poem talks about the realities of Caribbean islands — and how they differ from what the tourist sees of them. The islands are clearly important to the poet, but they're also a source of conflict.

You've Got to Know What the Poem's About

1) The narrator begins by challenging the stereotypical view tourists have of the islands.
2) She says that the islands are a real place with a long history — not just a holiday destination. She also implies that the islands are a difficult place to live.
3) She goes on to link the islands with members of her family. She describes some painful memories from living on the islands.
4) She finishes by expanding on the poem's title — poverty is the price paid by the islanders for the sun.

Learn About the Form, Structure and Language

1) **FORM** — The poem has short lines with non-standard grammar and not much punctuation — this makes it sound like the speech on the islands. There's some rhyme, but it's irregular. The first person narrator sounds like she's talking directly to you.
2) **STRUCTURE** — Each stanza has a distinct idea. The first is about the islands, the second is about the poet's personal feelings towards them and the third brings the poem to a conclusion.
3) **DIALECT** — The poem is written in a regional Caribbean dialect called patois — it's based on English, but it's non-standard. Using it shows the poet is proud of her culture and where she comes from.
4) **NATURAL IMAGERY** — She uses lots of powerful, natural images to describe the islands — she uses them to talk about the islands' age, as well as both their destructive power and their beauty.
5) **WORD PLAY** — Many words could have more than one meaning — it makes the poet's message more ambiguous, helping her to challenge people's perceptions.
6) **PERSONAL LANGUAGE** — She makes a lot of references to her family — it shows that the islands are part of her history and are important to her.

Remember the Feelings and Attitudes in the Poem

1) **CONFLICT** — The islands are important to her, but she also describes them as a difficult place to live. The islanders are poor and there's a lot of pain there — especially for her personally (her mother's cancer).
2) **CELEBRATION** — The use of local dialect is a celebration of the islands' culture. The poet seems proud of the age and history of the islands. She also wants to emphasise that there's more to them than what tourists see.

'We could definitely get it cheaper up the road...'

Go a Step Further and give a Personal Response

Have a go at answering these questions to help you come up with your own ideas about the poem:
Q1. How does the title turn out to be different to what we might expect?
Q2. Why do you think the poet wrote this poem in the Caribbean dialect?
Q3. Can you empathise with how the narrator feels towards her childhood home?

Themes — important places, relationships...

The narrator of 'Hard Water' also talks with pride about the area where she grew up — and uses dialect to do so. The 'Blackbird of Glanmore' is also about family relationships and home.

Gillian Clarke

Gillian Clarke was born in 1937 in Cardiff. She teaches creative writing at the University of Glamorgan. Many of her poems reflect her cultural identity and family relationships in Wales.

Neighbours

That spring was late. We watched the sky
and studied charts for shouldering isobars.
Birds were late to pair. Crows drank from the lamb's eye.

5 Over Finland small birds fell: song-thrushes
steering north, smudged signatures on light,
migrating warblers, nightingales.

Wing-beats failed over fjords, each lung a sip of gall.
Children were warned of their dangerous beauty.
Milk was spilt in Poland. Each quarrel

10 the blowback from some old story,
a mouthful of bitter air from the Ukraine
brought by the wind out of its box of sorrows.

This spring a lamb sips caesium on a Welsh hill.
A child, lifting her head to drink the rain,
15 takes into her blood the poisoned arrow.

Now we are all neighbourly, each little town
in Europe twinned to Chernobyl, each heart
with the burnt firemen, the child on the Moscow train.

In the democracy of the virus and the toxin
20 we wait. We watch for spring migrations,
one bird returning with green in its voice.

Glasnost. Golau glas. A first break of blue.

POEM DICTIONARY
isobar — a line on a weather map
gall — something bitter
Ukraine — Eastern European country, under Communist rule until 1991
caesium — a metal element, certain forms of which are radioactive
Chernobyl — a city in the Ukraine where a nuclear power plant exploded in 1986
Glasnost — a government policy in the USSR which encouraged honesty and openness
Golau glas — Welsh for 'blue light'

Section Two — Contemporary Poems

Neighbours

The poem is about the effects of the Chernobyl nuclear disaster in the late 1980s. Radioactive material released into the atmosphere was later found to have spread across Europe — even reaching Clarke's native Wales.

You've Got to Know What the Poem's About

1) In the first few stanzas, Clarke builds up tension by revealing the terrible after-effects of the disaster across Europe — but not what caused them.
2) The poem then jumps forward to the present and we find that the effects of the disaster have been both widespread and long-lasting.
3) It is not until the sixth stanza that Clarke specifically refers to Chernobyl. It's here that she also talks about the countries affected by the disaster being 'neighbours' — linked by the tragedy.
4) She finishes the poem by talking about hope for the future.

Learn About the Form, Structure and Language

1) **FORM** — The short stanzas make the poem look fragmented — this might echo the way the disaster was reported at the time. Enjambment between lines 9 and 10 suggests that the poet's thoughts might be disturbed or agitated.
2) **STRUCTURE** — The poem is a series of fragmented images and memories with no explicit connection between them. After the disaster no one really knew what was happening. You feel how confusing this must have been when you read the poem, because you have to piece together what it's about.
3) **TECHNICAL LANGUAGE** — This makes the poem more real and reminds us that these events actually happened. It also keeps the mood serious and sombre.
4) **CONTRASTS** — The poet contrasts springtime images of beauty and innocence with those of danger. This emphasises the terrible effects of the disaster.
5) **HOPEFUL LANGUAGE** — In the last few stanzas, the language becomes less bleak and more optimistic.
6) **IRONY** — The poet uses irony to show us that we are all neighbours whether we like it or not — and that democracy and sharing don't always bring good things.

Remember the Feelings and Attitudes in the Poem

1) **ANGER** — There's some fairly bitter language at the start of this poem, which suggests the poet is angry or upset about what happened. This is emphasised by the irony that the fallout affected everyone equally.
2) **HOPE** — The poem ends on a more hopeful note — that things will recover, spring will return and the future will be better. The disaster also showed that we care about our neighbours — a good thing.

Go a Step Further and give a Personal Response

Have a go at answering these questions to help you come up with your own ideas about the poem:
Q1. Why do you think this poem is called 'Neighbours'?
Q2. How is the feeling of tension built up in the first three stanzas?
Q3. How do you think the narrator feels about the disaster by the end of the poem?
Q4. Do you think the hope at the end of the poem is well-founded?

Themes — anger, hope...
The poems 'London' and 'A Vision' are also angry about a situation — but unlike Clarke, the poets offer no hope that the future will bring improvement.

Section Two — Contemporary Poems

Kathleen Jamie

Kathleen Jamie is a Scottish poet, now living in Fife. She studied at the University of Edinburgh and has since been 'writer-in-residence' at different universities. She has won several awards for her poetry since receiving the Creative Scotland award in 2001.

Crossing the Loch

Remember how we rowed toward the cottage
on the sickle-shaped bay,
that one night after the pub
loosed us through its swinging doors
5 and we pushed across the shingle
till water lipped the sides
as though the loch mouthed 'boat'?

I forget who rowed. Our jokes hushed.
The oars' splash, creak, and the spill
10 of the loch reached long into the night.
Out in the race I was scared:
the cold shawl of breeze,
and hunched hills; what the water held
of deadheads, ticking nuclear hulls.

15 Who rowed, and who kept their peace?
Who hauled salt-air and stars
deep into their lungs, were not reassured;
and who first noticed the loch's
phosphorescence, so, like a twittering nest
20 washed from the rushes, an astonished
small boat of saints, we watched water shine
on our fingers and oars,
the magic dart of our bow wave?

It was surely foolhardy, such a broad loch, a tide,
25 but we live – and even have children
to women and men we had yet to meet
that night we set out, calling our own
the sky and salt-water, wounded hills
dark-starred by blaeberries, the glimmering anklets
30 we wore in the shallows
as we shipped oars and jumped,
to draw the boat safe, high at the cottage shore.

POEM DICTIONARY
loch — Scottish lake
sickle-shaped — curved
shingle — gravel on a shore / beach
deadheads — logs half-sunk in water
phosphorescence — glow
blaeberries — Scottish word for bilberries

Crossing the Loch

The narrator is <u>reminiscing</u> about a <u>trip across a loch</u> that appears to have taken place a <u>long time ago</u> — before she grew up and had children. In it, she seems to be talking to the person or people she went on the trip with.

You've Got to Know What the Poem's About

1) The narrator is remembering a <u>rowing trip</u> across a loch which happened when she was <u>younger</u>.
2) She seems to be talking to someone who was <u>in the boat</u> with her at the time.
3) The trip appears to have been an <u>exciting</u> one — but also quite <u>scary</u>. It sounds like it's <u>night-time</u> and they're a bit drunk after leaving the pub.
4) The final stanza tells us that the trip happened a <u>long time ago</u> — the people in the boat have <u>grown up</u> and come a <u>long way</u> since then.

Learn About the Form, Structure and Language

1) **FORM** — The <u>first person narrator</u> in this poem could be the <u>poet</u> herself. There's <u>no rhyme scheme</u> or regular <u>rhythm</u> to the lines — perhaps to make it sound more <u>conversational</u>. The start of each stanza is <u>conversational</u>, but the poet isn't addressing us. She's talking to someone she <u>shares</u> the memory with.

2) **STRUCTURE** — The narrator begins with the people <u>leaving the pub</u> and the <u>excitement</u> of taking the boat out onto the loch. She remembers being <u>frightened</u>, but then she talks about the <u>magic</u> and <u>beauty</u> of the trip. She finishes by talking about <u>her life now</u> and the end of the boat trip.

3) **INTIMATE LANGUAGE** — This is used to <u>draw us in</u>, but also to <u>exclude</u> us. Jamie uses 'we' and 'our' a lot because she's really talking to the person who was in the boat with her.

4) **FRIGHTENING LANGUAGE** — The images in the second stanza feel quite <u>threatening</u> — this feeling is increased by the <u>personification</u> of the hills and water.

5) **MAGICAL LANGUAGE** — This language emphasises the <u>nostalgia</u> in the poem. This was probably a <u>magical time</u> in the life of the narrator — when she was younger and more adventurous. References to the <u>present</u> are more <u>matter of fact</u>.

Remember the Feelings and Attitudes in the Poem

1) **NOSTALGIA** — Crossing the loch is an event that the narrator seems to remember <u>fondly</u> — and one that still <u>means a lot</u> to her today. The person who crossed the loch with her was probably quite <u>special</u> to her.

2) **EXCITEMENT** — The narrator makes the trip sound <u>thrilling</u> — <u>scary</u>, but <u>fun</u>. This excitement may be something she feels is <u>missing</u> from her life today.

'Why did the chicken cross the loch?' was Alistair's favourite joke.

Go a Step Further and give a Personal Response

Have a go at <u>answering</u> these <u>questions</u> to help you come up with <u>your own ideas</u> about the poem:

Q1. How does the poet use language to involve the reader in the poem?
Q2. What impression do you get of the narrator's feelings as she looks back on this memory?
Q3. Do you think this poem is purely about a memory, or do you think there's more behind it?
Q4. What do you think the relationship is between the narrator and the person she's talking to?

Themes — memory, special places...

Many poems are about memories, including 'Cold Knap Lake', 'The Blackbird of Glanmore' and 'The Wild Swans at Coole'. These last two are also about places which are special to the poet.

Section Two — Contemporary Poems

Jean Sprackland

Jean Sprackland was born in Burton upon Trent, in the Midlands, in 1962, but now lives in Southport in Merseyside. Burton is famous for its breweries, which use the local water to brew the beer.

Hard Water

I tried the soft stuff on holiday in Wales,
a mania of teadrinking and hairwashing,
excitable soap which never rinsed away,

but I loved coming home to this.
5   Flat. Straight. Like the vowels,
like the straight talk: *hey up me duck*.
I'd run the tap with its swimming-pool smell,
get it cold and anaesthetic. Stand the glass
and let the little fizz of anxiety settle.
10 Honest water, bright and not quite clean.
The frankness of limestone, of gypsum,
the sour steam of cooling towers,
the alchemical taste of brewing.

On pitiless nights, I had to go for the bus
15 before last orders. I'd turn up my face,
let rain scald my eyelids and lips.
It couldn't lie. Fell thick
with a payload of acid. No salt –
this rain had forgotten the sea.
20 I opened my mouth, speaking nothing
in spite of my book-learning.
I let a different cleverness wash my tongue.
It tasted of work, the true taste
of early mornings, the blunt taste
25 of *don't get mardy*, of *too bloody deep for me*,
fierce lovely water that marked me for life
as belonging, regardless.

POEM DICTIONARY
hard water — water containing lots of minerals, characteristic of the Midlands
gypsum — a mineral
alchemical — changing things that aren't worth anything into something valuable
mardy — grumpy, sulky (Midlands dialect)

Section Two — Contemporary Poems

Hard Water

The narrator is talking about her love of the hard water in her home town. She links it to everything she loves about her local area — the language, the people and the way of life (even though this isn't always easy).

You've Got to Know What the Poem's About

1) The narrator describes the soft water she tried on holiday in Wales, which was fun and exciting.
2) She then says that she loves coming home to the hard water she's used to.
3) She compares the hard water to the local language and people, and links it to the industrial landscape of her home town. The qualities she gives the water — like honesty — are ones she values.
4) Life in her home town doesn't seem to always be easy — but she feels a loyalty to it anyway.
5) The poet is drawn to the water because it makes her feel at home.

Learn About the Form, Structure and Language

1) **FORM** — The use of the first person makes the poem sound personal and direct. There's no regular rhyme scheme or rhythm, maybe reflecting the down-to-earth way in which the local people talk.
2) **STRUCTURE** — The ideas in the poem are ordered to take us from carefree fun to gruff reality. The first stanza is full of the dizzy excitement of being on holiday, contrasting with the no-nonsense images in the second. In the final stanza, the dramatic tone returns, but now it seems unforgiving and painful.
3) **DIALECT** — The poet is proud of her roots — using phrases from the Midlands dialect is a celebration of where she comes from.
4) **STRAIGHTFORWARD LANGUAGE** — Her language is like that of the people around her — restrained and a bit blunt in places. She seems to value honesty and hard work, often linking the water to these qualities.
5) **CONTRASTS** — The poem contrasts 'excitable' soft water with the more serious, hard water of her local area. She uses a lot of industrial language to link hard water with her home town.

Remember the Feelings and Attitudes in the Poem

1) **PRIDE and BELONGING** — The poem celebrates the narrator's roots — she's proud of her home town and feels like she'll always belong there.
2) **VALUE of WATER** — Water is important to the poet's home town — it's used in the breweries which are the main industry there. The poet continually links the water to the local people and language.

Karen learnt never to mess with hard water.

Go a Step Further and give a Personal Response

Have a go at answering these questions to help you come up with your own ideas about the poem:

Q1. How is the Welsh water contrasted with hard water?
Q2. What does Sprackland seem to value about her local water?
Q3. How does she link the water to the people and landscape around her?
Q4. Would you like to live in the area she describes? Why / why not?

Themes — home, intense feelings...

The poem 'Price We Pay for the Sun' is about a significant place for the poet — her home. Other poems contain strong feelings about a place, for example, 'London' and 'Storm in the Black Forest'.

Section Three — Themes

Place

All the poems in this book are about different places — just in case it had escaped your attention. It's the one theme that links them all. The rest of this section will give you some ideas about other themes that link the poems — don't be afraid to come up with some more of your own though.

1) Poets often write about places — and the feelings and emotions they associate with them.
2) These places could be anywhere — a town, a country, a hillside, even a house.
3) Many places are important or significant in the life of the poet.

Home is often an Important place

Price We Pay for the Sun (Pages 26-27)

1) This poem is about the Caribbean islands where the narrator grew up.
2) The islands are an important part of her history. She shows how closely she's tied to them by linking the weather and landscape of the islands to members of her family: "my mother's breasts / like sleeping volcanoes".
3) The narrator seems proud to come from the islands, even though they're a difficult place to live. She celebrates their culture by writing in the local Caribbean dialect of Patois.

Hard Water (Pages 32-33)

1) This poem is a celebration of the poet's home town. Using phrases from the Midlands dialect — "hey up me duck", "don't get mardy" — suggests she's proud of her culture and her roots.
2) She links the properties of the town's hard water to the local language and the people. They share qualities she seems to value, like honesty and frankness.
3) The water in the town represents her sense of identity and belonging. She feels at home there and this seems important to her.

Hey up me duck.

Some places are associated with Special Memories

Crossing the Loch (Pages 30-31)

1) The poet is remembering a place where a significant event in her life took place.
2) The journey across the loch was special. It represents a time when she was young, brave and adventurous. She and her friends had their whole futures ahead of them.
3) The poet remembers this time and place fondly. She seems a bit nostalgic. Perhaps it's somewhere she wishes she could return to, but is unable to.

Other poems are also about special or important places...

'The Wild Swans at Coole' is also about a place that is significant to the poet, but his memories of it are bittersweet. In 'The Blackbird of Glanmore', the poet writes about his feelings on coming home.

Place

The entire cluster is called "Place" — so, as you might expect, there are lots of variations on the theme...

Sometimes a place Changes Us

Below the Green Corrie (Pages 12-13)

1) The poet says that the mountains in this poem have "enriched" his life.
2) The mountains are great and powerful. They give up some of this power to the poet when they fill him with their "thunders".
3) The mountains change the poet's life for the better. He seems grateful for his experience of them.

Finding this little lot while out walking really did enrich Norm's life.

The Prelude (Pages 8-9)

1) The narrator has his view of the world changed by a dramatic encounter with a mountain.
2) To begin with, he's happy and confident, but the encounter changes him — he's left "in grave / And serious mood". The effect is long lasting.
3) His outlook on life is turned completely upside down by this event. The world around him appears different — he's no longer sure of himself.

Some places are Bleak or Depressing

London (Pages 4-5)

1) Blake doesn't like what he sees as he walks through the streets of London.
2) This urban landscape is full of misery and suffering. The language he uses to describe the city is dark and dramatic, e.g. "black'ning church", "Runs in blood".
3) There seems to be no escape from the relentless horror around him.
4) The poet gives the impression that the whole city is like this — "each chartered street" — and that every section of society is affected — "palace-walls", "chimney-sweeper's cry".

A Vision (Pages 20-21)

1) People once had visions of the future as the ideal place to live. In this poem, today is that future and the reality is very different.
2) The present is harsh and bleak — old dreams of beauty and perfection were never realised.
3) The dreams are made to seem childish and fake, all "fairground rides" and "fuzzy-felt grass".
4) This contrasts with the stark, realistic images of the present, e.g. "north wind", "landfill site".

Other poems touch on these themes too...

In 'Neighbours', the poet paints a bleak picture of the world after a disaster but ends hopefully. Like 'London', 'Price We Pay for the Sun' tells about the hardships of a particular place.

Section Three — Themes

Nature

The natural world comes up quite a lot in poems about place.

> 1) The beauty and power of nature can be exciting.
> 2) Nature can also be violent and destructive.
> 3) Nature needs to be treated with respect and not taken for granted.

Nature can be Magical or Mysterious

Spellbound (Pages 10-11)

1) The storm in this poem is like a magic spell — it has an invisible hold over the narrator.
2) Nature is dark and dangerous, but also thrilling — the narrator is entranced by it.
3) Natural images are idyllic, but also threatening — "bare boughs weighed with snow".
4) The narrator is so captivated by the storm's power, she's unable to leave despite the danger.

Crossing the Loch (Pages 30-31)

1) The language the poet uses to describe the loch makes it sound beautiful and otherworldly. She talks about the water's "phosphorescence" and a "boat of saints". The water's glow is mysterious and unexplained.
2) Nature is made to seem magical and exciting — but it's also frightening. The narrator admits to being "scared".

Ooh look, wild swans.
Wrong poem, love.

It can also be Awe-Inspiring

Below the Green Corrie (Pages 12-13)

1) The mountains in this poem are personified as brash, swaggering "bandits".
2) This imagery makes the mountains seem heroic and exciting — like characters from a film. It also gives them a dangerous and slightly threatening edge.
3) The narrator's tone and language suggest he's in awe of the mountains' power.
4) He knows they're dangerous as well as fun — and capable of causing harm. Perhaps this danger is what makes them so exciting.

The Prelude (Pages 8-9)

1) At first, the narrator sees nature as a series of pretty, unthreatening images. He seems happy and carefree and his tone is light and unafraid.
2) But the appearance of the mountain changes all this. The "huge peak" is personified — it's calm and powerful, "with purpose of its own". Nature has become darker and much more sinister — and the narrator becomes scared and deeply in awe of it.
3) Bringing the mountain to life makes the narrator's fear seem more real and understandable. It helps the reader to empathise with his terror.

Other poems are about the magic of nature...

In 'Storm in the Black Forest', the storm itself is made to sound mysterious and exciting — nature and its power seem to inspire awe in the eyes of the narrator too.

Section Three — Themes

Nature

Poets do love a bit of nature — here are some more nature-related themes...

Nature is often Powerful

Wind (Pages 16-17)

1) The storm in this poem is violent and destructive.
2) It's so powerful, it's as if it has the strength to move mountains: "The hills had new places".
3) Nothing can escape the damage — especially the vulnerable house.
4) The humans in the poem are completely powerless to control or stop the storm.

Storm in the Black Forest (Pages 14-15)

1) The narrator of this poem describes witnessing an amazing lightning storm.
2) The storm's power is electrifying — it's wild, and seemingly untameable.
3) The narrator questions people's belief that they can control this power.
4) Through his mockery, mankind is made to seem arrogant and foolish for ever thinking that they had "mastered" electricity.

The Moment (Pages 22-23)

1) In this poem, nature has lulled humans into a false sense of security — allowing us to believe that we are in control of our lives and the world around us.
2) But nature is capable of taking away everything we own — even the air we breathe. Nature has the real power and we "own nothing".
3) The poet shows us many sides to nature — it can be violent and angry ("the cliffs fissure and collapse") or quiet and calm ("No, they whisper").
4) She seems to suggest that we underestimate nature, when we should fear and respect it for the damage it can cause.

Ahh look. Nature isn't mean at all.

It can be Beautiful

The Wild Swans at Coole (Pages 6-7)

1) The narrator describes the swans as "brilliant creatures" and "Mysterious, beautiful".
2) He talks about them with great love and admiration. He clearly respects them.
3) The "autumn beauty" of the scene around him is also carefully described. The poem seems partly to be a celebration of the poet's love of nature in general.

Other poems are about the power of nature...

The power of nature is also written about in 'Below the Green Corrie' and 'The Prelude'. Nature's destructive power and its effects on humans are also touched upon in 'Price We Pay for the Sun'.

Section Three — Themes

Memory

Lots of poets write about the feelings and uncertainties associated with memories.

> 1) Memories can trigger different thoughts and feelings.
> 2) Some memories are unreliable — we may not always remember things exactly.

Some memories Make Us Think about our lives

The Blackbird of Glanmore (Pages 18-19)

1) The sight of a blackbird at his family home makes the poet remember his younger brother who died as a child. The bright, lively bird seems to link with the boy in the poet's mind.
2) The bird and the memories of his brother make the poet contemplate his own death and mortality — "I've a bird's eye view of myself, / A shadow raked on gravel".
3) This poem also makes the reader reflective. The rhythm slows in the second stanza with the line "Breathe. Just breathe and sit". The poet seems to be encouraging us to sit and remember with him.

The Wild Swans at Coole (Pages 6-7)

1) The narrator remembers seeing the swans the first time he was at Coole and it makes him reflective.
2) It's been a long time since his first visit and since then "All's changed" for him. He's old and weary and his "heart is sore". The swans still seem the same though — lively and full of youth.
3) His memories of the swans seem to make the narrator aware of his age and the things he may be missing in his life — like love and companionship.

Sometimes memories can be Uncertain

Cold Knap Lake (Pages 24-25)

1) The narrator uses this poem to explore the nature of memory and questions its reliability.
2) Her memories seem clear and vivid to begin with, but they become murky and confused.
3) The narrator can't be sure if the event she's describing is real or made up. She links the "troubled surface" of the lake to the uncertainty of distant memories. Words like "shadowy" and "satiny" make her descriptions sound dreamy and vague — like the memories themselves.
4) She seems to conclude that all memories are like this though. Maybe it doesn't matter if some details get imagined.

Crossing the Loch (Pages 30-31)

1) In places, the narrator seems uncertain of particular details: "I forget who rowed".
2) She asks questions of the person she's speaking to: "who kept their peace?"
3) But certain parts of the trip are clearly and vividly described. The magic and excitement of the journey have stayed in the poet's mind — perhaps these overall feelings are more important to her than specific and relatively minor details.

Um, who's actually rowing?

Other poems feature the theme of memory...

In 'Price We Pay for the Sun', the narrator seems to be remembering her childhood on the islands. In 'A Vision', the narrator remembers how people in the past used to view and plan for the future.

Section Three — Themes

Sadness

Not all the themes in these poems are positive ones. Well, you can't be happy all the time...

> 1) Some poets are sad or disappointed by a place or situation they think needs improving.
> 2) Some are sad about events that have happened in their own life — like the death of a loved one.

Some poets are Sad About a Place

London (Pages 4-5)

1) Blake is in despair about the state of London and the people who live there.
2) He emphasises the misery in the city by linking contrasting images of innocence and joy with those of desperation and sadness: "Blasts the new-born infant's tear".
3) He also links happiness and death with the image of the "marriage hearse". This seems to suggest that the cycle of despair will only continue as people marry and have children.

A Vision (Pages 20-21)

1) The poet begins by describing designs for a future that is bright and exciting.
2) But this future was consigned to the "landfill site". Despite the optimism of the people making the plans, no one ever got to live in the perfect future town.
3) The sharp contrast between the dream and the reality creates a feeling of sadness — the idealistic futures are "unlived in".

As soon as Mark had a vision of winning the lottery, he went out and bought himself a new car.

Others are more Personally Sad

The Blackbird of Glanmore (Pages 18-19)

1) The feeling of sadness in this poem comes from the poet's thoughts of his brother's death.
2) This feeling is emphasised by the poet's use of contrasting images. He creates a happy, carefree picture of his brother "Cavorting through the yard" and follows it with the bleakness of "the accident".
3) Further contrasts come from the poignant images of the "stillness dancer" and "Haunter-son" — a much-loved little boy, full of life and movement, has become a still, silent ghost.
4) The images seem to emphasise the poet's feelings that his brother shouldn't have died. By creating them, the poet is reminding us of the difference between past and present. It makes it easy for us to share his sadness over the death and empathise with him.

Other poems feature the theme of sadness...

The tone of 'The Wild Swans at Coole' is quite sad as the narrator seems to reflect on his life. 'Neighbours' also seems sad in places, when the poet writes about the effects of the disaster.

Section Three — Themes

Uncertainty

Another cheery theme. Don't worry, they pick up a bit after this.

> 1) Some poets write about uncertainty — and the fear and confusion it can bring.
> 2) Sometimes they write about being confident one minute and uncertain the next — and how it feels to lose confidence.

Some Poems are about the Narrator's Loss of Certainty

The Prelude (Pages 8-9)

1) At the start of this extract, the narrator appears certain of himself and his place in the world.
2) He's almost arrogant in this certainty — "Proud of his skill", "lustily / I dipped my oars".
3) But the appearance of the mountain robs him of all this.
4) The mountain shows him nature's dark, powerful edge — he's troubled and confused by it: "huge and mighty forms, that do not live / Like living men". The mountain seemed alive to him, but he doesn't know how this could be possible.

Cold Knap Lake (Pages 24-25)

1) The narrator's tale is confidently told to start with.
2) She seems sure of the details — her mother "kneeling", the drowned child's blue lips.
3) But suddenly, she loses her certainty. The language she uses becomes vague and dreamlike — "shadowy", "cloudiness" — and her sentences become long and trailing.
4) She doesn't know which parts of her story, if any, are real.

Some Poems cause Uncertainty in the Reader

Anna had a bit of a moment when she remembered she'd left the iron on.

The Moment (Pages 22-23)

1) In the first stanza, the poet describes the reader as being certain that they're in control of their life: "you stand in the centre of your room / ... and say, I own this".
2) But the poet shocks us with a sudden change of tone in the second stanza, quickly making us realise that this isn't true. We've taken everything we think we own from the natural world — and it could easily be taken back.
3) The poet seems to be trying to rob the reader of his or her certainty — "You own nothing" — perhaps to change the way we view the world.

Other poems feature the theme of uncertainty...

In 'Price We Pay for the Sun', the narrator appears uncertain of what her feelings towards her homeland should be. In contrast, the narrator of 'London' is very certain of his view of the city.

Section Three — Themes

Relationships

I'm not just talking about the stuff of dating websites and teen problem pages here — and neither are our poets. We have all sorts of different relationships.

> 1) Relationships don't necessarily have to be romantic.
> 2) They're the connections we have with the people and places we know well.
> 3) They can be loving or cruel, and make us happy or sad. They're often quite complicated.

Some relationships are Loving

The Blackbird of Glanmore (Pages 18-19)

1) This poem is about a blackbird and how it reminds the narrator of his relationship with his brother.
2) The narrator is explicit about his love for the bird — "It's you, blackbird, I love".
   His description of it is warm and affectionate — "Hedge-hop", "Filling the stillness with life".
3) But his love is tinged with sadness — it's linked to his love for his brother.
4) The relationship is a fragile one. The bird is "ready to scare off / At the very first wrong move". Perhaps the poet feels that all relationships are as delicate and easily lost as this one.

Some relationships are Long-Distance

Neighbours (Pages 28-29)

1) One of the main themes of this poem is that we are closer than we think to the people of far-off countries. Whether we like it or not, we are all "Neighbours" and linked together.
2) The Chernobyl disaster shows us this — countries across Europe were affected by it. The spread of radioactive material didn't respect borders, even reaching "a Welsh hill".
3) But being "neighbourly" also means caring for those around us. The people of Chernobyl were strangers and a long way away — but people felt close to them, and sympathised with them.

Some relationships are Confusing

Price We Pay for the Sun (Pages 26-27)

1) The narrator seems to have conflicting emotions about the islands where she grew up. Her relationship with them is a complicated one.
2) The islands are important to her. She seems to feel a kind of fierce pride about them when she challenges the stereotypical views of the tourists.
3) But, "these islands split / bone" — life for the people who live on them can be hard and poverty-stricken. The islands are also a place of personal pain and grief for the poet — her mum may well have died there after suffering from cancer.
4) The narrator seems to feel confused about her relationship with the islands — they hurt her, but they also pull her back. The last line, "run come", suggests she doesn't know whether to stay or go.

Other poems feature the theme of relationships...
In 'Below the Green Corrie', the poet writes about his relationship with the mountains and the bond he forms with them. The poem 'Wind' may be a metaphor for a troubled romantic relationship.

Section Three — Themes

Passion

Passion doesn't necessarily have to have anything to do with <u>love</u> or <u>lust</u>.

> 1) Passion means having <u>intense</u> or <u>powerful feelings</u> towards something.
> 2) These feelings could be anything from <u>excitement</u> to <u>anger</u>.

Many of the poems are full of Intense Feelings

Storm in the Black Forest (Pages 14-15)

1) The <u>irregular layout</u> of this poem suggests it was written <u>spontaneously</u> and <u>passionately</u>.
2) The language is also <u>passionate</u>. It sounds <u>natural</u> and <u>instinctive</u> — "bronzey soft sky".
3) <u>Repetition</u> of phrases makes the narrator sound <u>caught up</u> in the moment — as if he's saying the words as they occur to him — "pure white liquid fire, bright white... brighter white".
4) Much of the language is <u>onomatopoeic</u> — "tipples", "cackles". It helps bring the description <u>alive</u>.
5) <u>Exclamation marks</u> add to the <u>intensity</u> of feeling in the final lines. The narrator sounds <u>scornful</u> and almost <u>angry</u> at mankind's vanity.

Spellbound (Pages 10-11)

1) The narrator of this poem is <u>passionate</u> about a <u>storm</u>.
2) <u>Repetition</u> of words, "cannot, cannot go", suggests she's <u>caught up</u> in the <u>excitement</u> of the moment. It also adds to the <u>intensity</u> of the poem.
3) The <u>rhythm</u> and <u>rhyme scheme</u> make the poem sound like a <u>chant</u>. The storm is casting a <u>spell</u> over the narrator — she feels "bound", as if by a "tyrant".

Hard Water (Pages 32-33)

1) The narrator of this poem is <u>passionate</u> about her <u>home town</u> and its <u>people</u>.
2) She shows her feelings for the area through her <u>enthusiastic</u> descriptions and <u>praise</u> of the local <u>water</u> which has parallel qualities — "I loved coming home to this".
3) Even though the town sounds <u>hard</u> and <u>industrial</u> — "the sour steam of cooling towers", "pitiless nights" — the narrator speaks about it with <u>affection</u> and <u>pride</u>. She's <u>happy</u> she belongs there.

Some poets are Passionately Angry

London (Pages 4-5)

1) The poet seems <u>angry</u> that those in <u>power</u> do <u>nothing</u> to help the people of London.
2) At first, his tone seems <u>neutral</u> — "I wander" — as if he's just describing what he sees. He doesn't <u>explicitly</u> show his anger.
3) But his <u>powerful</u>, <u>emotive</u> images <u>convey</u> this anger to the reader — "mind-forged manacles", "harlot's curse", "blights with plagues".
4) This language <u>emphasises</u> the sheer <u>strength</u> of the poet's feelings. He wants us to feel as <u>shocked</u> and <u>appalled</u> by the situation as he does.

Other poems feature intense feelings...

In the poem 'Wind', the language is intense and dramatic — we feel the real fear of the people in the house. 'The Moment' also builds in intensity as we witness the power and violence of nature.

Section Three — Themes

Hope

Ah, what a lovely theme to end this section on...

> 1) Some poets find hope in the most difficult situations.
> 2) Some situations are so bad, it feels like there is no hope.

Some poems seem to have No Hope

Wind (Pages 16-17)

1) Throughout this poem we're given images of the storm's power, e.g. "wind that dented the balls of my eyes".
2) The storm seems unrelenting — nothing can escape its path. Some of the damage may well be irreparable.
3) You might expect the storm to finish at the end of the poem, but the last lines give us no sign it will be over anytime soon.
4) The people in the house have no choice but to "sit on" and wait it out. They're powerless to do anything else.

Learn to embrace the wind.

A Vision (Pages 20-21)

1) This poem begins by talking about people's hopes for the future.
2) But sadly, these hopes turn out to be false. The plans they were based on have little to do with reality — "fuzzy-felt grass" and "board-game suburbs" were too perfect to ever be achieved.
3) The poet also hints that the planners believed in the American Dream — he talks about them doing typically American activities like catching "the late show" and "strolling the boulevard". The American Dream was about achieving a better life for everyone, but many people have said it's unrealistic and impossible to achieve.
4) All hope seems to have been extinguished by the end of the poem — the future is now "fully extinct". This particular dream will never be achieved.

Others are More Optimistic

Neighbours (Pages 28-29)

1) This poem is about the damage caused by the Chernobyl disaster in 1986 — a pretty bleak topic. There are images of death and destruction throughout. Despite this, the poem ends on a hopeful note.
2) The poet suggests that the disaster has made us more aware of our neighbours. We care about "the child on the Moscow train", even though they're far away.
3) The last line of the poem is the most hopeful of all. The "first break of blue" suggests the return of spring, new life, and recovery from the disaster.
4) The link between "Glasnost" and "Golau glas" also suggests a hopefulness about the political situation in the Ukraine.

Other poems feature the theme of hope...

The narrator in 'The Blackbird of Glanmore' reflects on sad events and his own mortality, but the end of the poem is bright and optimistic. In 'London', the poet offers no hope for a better future.

Section Three — Themes

Poetic Forms

As well as themes and ideas, you have to be able to write about technical stuff like form and structure too.

> 1) Form is the type of poem and its features.
> 2) It's used to create different moods and effects.
> 3) You have to be able to write about how these effects are created.

Some poetic forms are Pretty Strict

London (Pages 4-5)

1) This poem is written in quatrains, making it seem formal and carefully constructed. Each quatrain covers a new but related point.
2) It seems the poet has thought quite a lot about what he wants to say — this gives the impression that he has an important message to get across to the reader.
3) The regular rhythm (iambic tetrameter) puts a strong stress on key words like "fear" and "sigh", making them stand out.

The Wild Swans at Coole (Pages 6-7)

1) This poem has quite a controlled form — there are five stanzas of equal length, a reasonably consistent iambic rhythm and a regular ABCBDD rhyme scheme.
2) This helps to give the poem its calm, measured and reflective tone.
3) The poem's full of emotion — "And now my heart is sore" — but it's contained by the regular form. The emotion is understated, but possibly more powerful because of it. It makes the narrator appear thoughtful, rather than self-pitying.

Others are Less Strict

Storm in the Black Forest (Pages 14-15)

1) This poem appears wild and chaotic — perhaps echoing the experience of the storm itself.
2) The lines and stanzas vary in length and there is no regular rhythm or rhyme scheme.
3) This makes the poem sound natural and spontaneous. It also allows the poet to emphasise the strength of his feelings in short lines like "supposed to!"
4) A more controlled form would make it harder to convey the narrator's passion and excitement.

A Vision (Pages 20-21)

1) There is some pattern to the form of this poem. The lines are all ten syllables long and look tidy and regular on the page. This could be to echo the neat "blueprints" in the future plans. The lines are also neatly arranged in quatrains.
2) There's no rhyme scheme though, which makes the poem sound natural and informal. This fits in with the poem's conversational tone.

You can write about the form of any poem...

'The Moment' and 'Price We Pay for the Sun' both have irregular forms, with varying line lengths and no fixed rhythm or rhyme scheme. This makes them sound natural and quite conversational.

Poetic Devices and Structure

There are loads of poetic devices you could talk about, but this page gives you a few examples.

1) Poetic devices are techniques that allow a poet to create different moods and effects.
2) Structure is about the order of ideas in a poem — and the effect this produces.

Devices include Enjambment, Caesura and Repetition

The Blackbird of Glanmore (Pages 18-19)

1) Enjambment helps this poem to sound thoughtful and natural — which in turn helps us to empathise with the feelings of the narrator.
2) Caesura is used to draw the reader in, "Breathe. Just breathe and sit". It slows the pace of the poem and invites us to sit and reflect along with the narrator.

Spellbound (Pages 10-11)

1) Repetition of certain words makes this poem sound like a chant or spell: "I cannot, cannot go... / And yet I cannot go... / I will not, cannot go".
2) This links to the title of the poem and emphasises the impression that the narrator has been hypnotised by the storm.

A Vision (Pages 20-21)

1) Enjambment is part of this poem's relaxed form — sentences run from one line to the next and across stanzas.
2) By including us in his thoughts, the narrator may be trying to encourage us to agree with him.

Structure is about Organising Ideas

The Moment (Pages 22-23)

1) The order of ideas in this poem is particularly important.
2) It starts with the calm confidence of human beings, "you stand in the centre of your room, / ...and say, *I own this*".
3) It then shocks us with nature's power and violence — "the cliffs fissure and collapse" — to emphasise the difference between our view of the world and reality.

Crossing the Loch (Pages 30-31)

1) This is a narrative poem — so it's told like a proper story.
2) There's a clear beginning, middle and end. Events are recalled in the order they happened in.
3) This allows the poet to guide us through her different emotions — from excitement in the first stanza, to uncertainty, then wonder, and finally a sense of reflection to end the poem.

You can write about the structure of any poem...

The structure of 'Cold Knap Lake' is important — the tone is bold and confident to begin with, but becomes vague and confused as she starts to question her memories.

Section Four — Poetry Techniques

Beginnings of Poems

Begin at the beginning, that's what I always say...

1) The beginning of a poem is really important — a good opening will draw the reader in.
2) A beginning can be used to set the scene or tone for the poem.
3) Sometimes the start of a poem has a contrasting mood or tone to the end of the poem.

Beginnings can be used to Set the Scene

Crossing the Loch (Pages 30-31)

1) The first stanza tells us how the trip across the loch began. It sets the scene for the story.
2) The stanza is one long sentence, which draws the reader into the narrative.
3) But the opening phrase "Remember how we rowed" also tells us that the narrator isn't really talking to us. She's addressing the person she shares the memory with.

Not everyone is impressed by visual metaphors.

Wind (Pages 16-17)

1) The clear visual metaphor in the opening line — "This house has been far out at sea all night" — helps us to easily imagine the scene the poet is describing.
2) Straight away, we get a feeling for the storm's power — and the narrator's vulnerability to it. These ideas are then explored in more detail.

Neighbours (Pages 28-29)

1) The abrupt opening sentence sets an ominous tone — "That spring was late." It draws the reader in by making them question what's going on.
2) The line is followed by a series of unsettling, fragmented images — "Birds were late to pair. Crows drank from the lamb's eye." These give clues as to what the poem's about and build up the tension.
3) This first stanza has a dark, fearful air and sets a sombre mood for the rest of the poem. This seems appropriate for such a serious subject.

Sometimes beginnings Contrast with the Rest of the Poem

Below the Green Corrie (Pages 12-13)

1) The tone in the opening stanza seems dark and a little threatening. The mountains "gathered round... / full of thunders".
2) But the mountains surprise us by giving up on their threats.
3) The rest of the poem is lighter and more affectionate in tone.

Lots of poems have interesting beginnings...

The pretty, peaceful scene at the beginning of 'The Prelude' is a stark contrast to the dark, ominous tones of the narrator at the end of the extract — almost the opposite of 'Below the Green Corrie'.

Section Four — Poetry Techniques

Couplets and Last Lines

Endings are just as important as beginnings — a good one will leave a lasting impression on the reader.

> 1) Last lines can be used to sum up or round off a poem.
> 2) Sometimes they provide a neat conclusion — and sometimes they leave us with more questions.

Last lines can Sum Up the Poem

Price We Pay for the Sun (Pages 26-27)

1) The last three lines of the poem emphasise the poet's point. The islanders pay the real price for the sun — poverty.
2) These last lines sound direct and matter of fact. They sum up the message of the poem.
3) The poet still leaves us with some uncertainty. The meaning of the final line, "run come", is unclear — perhaps because the narrator herself is unclear about whether to stay or go.

Hard Water (Pages 32-33)

1) The final two lines of this poem sum up why the water means so much to the poet — it connects her to her home town, giving her a feeling of "belonging".
2) The tone in these two lines seems serious and heartfelt — the poet is revealing the true extent of her emotions.
3) This allows a more personal feeling of empathy towards the poet and a deeper understanding of why she wrote the poem.
4) The contradictory description of "fierce lovely water" shows her unconventional but strongly held affection.

Last lines can Throw Doubt on things

Cold Knap Lake (Pages 24-25)

It's far too cold to be having a nap out here.

1) The final two lines form the only rhyming couplet in the poem — this adds impact to the poet's closing statement.
2) She uses the couplet to bring the poem to a neat conclusion — memories are unreliable and can't be trusted.
3) These final lines, like the opening ones, have a very definite tone. But her certainty at the beginning comes from feeling confident in her knowledge — the narrator's certainty at the end comes from realising that she doesn't really know anything.
4) The fact that the memory lies "under closing water" suggests she'll never get her full memory back, so the poem ends with a sense of loss.

You can write about the endings of any poem...

The last line of 'Neighbours' is significant, because it offers hope at the end of quite a bleak poem. In 'Spellbound', the ending suggests for the first time that the narrator is choosing to stick around.

Section Four — Poetry Techniques

Rhyme and Rhythm

It's important to be able to say <u>why</u> you think a poet has picked a particular rhythm or rhyme scheme — or <u>why</u> you think they've chosen <u>not to use</u> them.

> 1) <u>Rhyme</u> and <u>rhythm</u> affect a poem's <u>mood</u> or <u>atmosphere</u>.
> 2) They can make it sound <u>happy</u> and <u>cheerful</u>, <u>sad</u> or <u>angry</u>, <u>dull</u> or <u>magical</u>.
> 3) Their <u>absence</u> can also affect how a poem sounds.

Rhyme and rhythm are used to Create Effects

Spellbound (Pages 10-11)

1) The <u>regular ABAB rhyme</u> and <u>iambic rhythm</u> in this poem make it sound like a <u>song</u>, e.g. "The giant trees are bending... / And the storm is fast descending". This makes it memorable to <u>listen to</u> or <u>say out loud</u>.
2) Perhaps the <u>noise of the storm</u> is a bit like a song or a chant and that's what's <u>casting a spell</u> over the narrator. This could be what's <u>reflected</u> in the poem.

London (Pages 4-5)

1) The <u>constant rhyme</u> and <u>rhythm</u> in this poem help to emphasise the <u>unrelenting suffering</u> in the city.
2) They're very <u>consistent</u>, which gives a feeling of <u>order</u> and <u>clarity</u> to the words. The regular <u>ABAB</u> rhyme scheme helps us to <u>focus</u> on the poet's <u>message</u>.
3) This consistency also helps the narrator to sound more <u>plausible</u>. He seems to be <u>in control</u> of his words, having thought carefully about what he wants to say. This makes his message appear more <u>serious</u> and more <u>believable</u>.

Lack of rhyme or rhythm also Creates an Effect

The Moment (Pages 22-23)

1) The <u>absence</u> of a regular rhyme scheme or rhythm helps to <u>emphasise</u> this poem's <u>powerful message</u>.
2) The lack of a fixed rhythm helps the poet to create <u>different moods</u> and <u>tones</u>.
3) E.g. The long list of places in <u>line 4</u> sounds <u>breathless</u> and <u>excited</u> — as if the narrator is getting carried away. This <u>contrasts</u> with the <u>slower</u>, measured rhythm of <u>line 13</u> — perhaps this is to show that <u>nature</u> is <u>calmer</u> and more <u>rational</u> than humans.

What they lacked in rhythm, Sheila and Dave made up for in sheer flexibility.

Other poems contain rhyme and rhythm...

'The Wild Swans at Coole' has a regular ABCBDD rhyme scheme, making it sound carefully thought out. The lack of rhyme in 'Storm in the Black Forest' makes it sound spontaneous, like the storm.

Section Four — Poetry Techniques

Use of the First Person

The narrative voice makes a big difference to a poem.

> 1) A first person narrator talks from their own point of view, using words like "I" and "me".
> 2) A narrator who uses the second person talks to somebody else, using the word "you".
> 3) A third person narrator commentates on events using words like "she" and "they".
> 4) First person narration tends to be quite personal. Third person narration is often more detached and objective.

First Person Narrators make a poem feel more Personal

The Blackbird of Glanmore (Pages 18-19)

1) The first person narrator in this poem is probably the poet himself. He's thinking about the death of his younger brother — a personal and emotional subject.
2) Speaking in the first person makes the poem more intimate and emotive — "And I think of one gone to him / A... / lost brother".
3) We feel like we're hearing the thoughts of a real person and so we're able to empathise more with the narrator's feelings.

Hard Water (Pages 32-33)

1) This poem is about a subject that's close to the poet's heart.
2) She's sharing with us her personal feelings towards her home town — "I tried the soft stuff on holiday... / but I loved coming home to this".
3) Using the town's water as a symbol for the area might seem like an unusual approach, but using a first person narrator makes it more understandable and moving.
4) It also adds to the conversational tone of the poem.

Hard water

Not All poems are in the First Person

The Moment (Pages 22-23)

1) This poem criticises human beings and their failings.
2) It can do this effectively because the narrator addresses us in the second person, using "you". This makes it seem quite argumentative. It sounds almost factual when the narrator says, "the air moves back from you... / and you can't breathe".
3) The narrative voice makes the poem scarier and more convincing.

Other poems use first person narrators...

The first person narrator of 'A Vision' doesn't start using the word 'I' until the end of the poem. This makes the whole thing feel suddenly personal and more real — as if it actually happened.

Section Four — Poetry Techniques

Imagery

The language a poet uses helps us <u>picture</u> what's happening. This is called <u>imagery</u>.

> 1) Imagery helps the reader to <u>imagine</u> the situations, places, people and emotions described in a poem.
> 2) Poets often use <u>metaphors</u> and <u>similes</u> to describe things.

Imagery helps us to Imagine things

Below the Green Corrie (Pages 12-13)

1) The poet compares the mountains he's walking in to a group of "<u>bandits</u>". It's an <u>effective image</u> because it can be <u>interpreted</u> in <u>different ways</u>.
2) To begin with, the image makes the mountains appear <u>intimidating</u> and possibly <u>dangerous</u> — they "gathered round" and "swaggered up close". They come across as a bit <u>thuggish</u>.
3) But then the <u>tone changes</u> — the bandits become "swashbuckling" heroes, <u>fun</u> and <u>adventurous</u>. The mountains are made to seem <u>wild</u> but <u>friendly</u>.
4) The bandit imagery gives the mountains <u>character</u> and <u>personality</u> — it brings them alive. It also highlights that there are <u>two sides</u> to them — <u>danger</u> and <u>exhilaration</u>.

Wind (Pages 16-17)

My house is quite vulnerable to the wind. I don't know why.

1) The <u>imagery</u> in this poem illustrates the <u>sheer strength</u> of the wind and the <u>vulnerability</u> of the house and the people in it.
2) The wind is <u>personified</u> to seem cruel, violent and full of <u>human aggression</u> — "The wind flung a magpie away".
3) The <u>house</u> is made to seem <u>treasured</u> and <u>important</u>, but <u>easily broken</u> — like a "fine green goblet".
4) These images might also suggest a <u>double meaning</u> to the poem. The <u>wind</u> could be a metaphor for an <u>argument</u> between two people and the <u>house</u> could represent their <u>relationship</u> — about to be <u>destroyed</u> by the force of the row.

Imagery can Affect a poem's Mood

The Prelude (Pages 8-9)

1) To begin with, the scene is set using <u>beautiful</u> and <u>picturesque images</u>: "A little boat tied to a willow tree", "sparkling light", "elfin pinnace".
2) The <u>mood</u> is <u>peaceful</u> and <u>idyllic</u> — the narrator seems <u>happy</u> and <u>carefree</u>.
3) But the <u>ugly image</u> of the mountain's "grim shape" as it "Upreared its head" <u>changes the mood</u> completely. The poem becomes much <u>darker</u> and <u>more chilling</u>.

Most poems contain imagery...

'Price We Pay for the Sun' contains a lot of natural imagery to help us imagine the islands. The poet also uses it to link the islands with her family, showing us how important they both are to her.

Section Four — Poetry Techniques

Language Features

Language is obviously a pretty darn important part of any poem.

> 1) Language features can make a poet's <u>feelings</u> more <u>forceful</u> or <u>convincing</u>.
> 2) They can also be used to help create <u>vivid pictures</u> in the reader's mind.

Some poets use Dialect to show their Identity

Price We Pay for the Sun (Pages 26-27)

1) The poet's use of the <u>Caribbean dialect</u> suggests she's <u>proud</u> of <u>who she is</u> and <u>where she's from</u> — one of the poem's main subjects.
2) The patois dialect makes the narrator sound <u>authentic</u> and <u>believable</u> — we're prepared to accept that she <u>knows</u> what she's <u>talking about</u> when she opens with "These islands / not picture postcards...".
3) The poet is also quite <u>creative</u> with her language and often <u>plays with words</u> — e.g. "<u>unravelling tourists</u>" could be about tourists relaxing and <u>unwinding</u>, or it could be a more <u>perceptive comment</u> about them being under stress and losing their composure.

Hard Water (Pages 32-33)

1) The poet uses <u>local dialect</u> phrases like "mardy" and "hey up me duck" with <u>pride</u> and <u>affection</u>. In doing so, she's <u>celebrating</u> the area she comes from.
2) The phrases seem to give her a sense of <u>identity</u>. Using them is a bit like using a <u>secret code</u> — understanding the code gives her a feeling of <u>belonging</u>.

Others use Sound Effects

Wind (Pages 16-17)

1) The poet uses some very <u>effective images</u> to help us <u>visualise</u> the powerful <u>storm</u>.
2) But to give us a <u>better sense</u> of its <u>power</u>, he also tries to <u>recreate</u> how it <u>sounds</u> using <u>onomatopoeic language</u> like "booming", "drummed" and "rang".
3) <u>Alliteration</u> in the second stanza, "<u>w</u>ind <u>w</u>ielded", "<u>B</u>lade-<u>l</u>ight, <u>l</u>uminous <u>b</u>lack", helps to build up the <u>drama</u> and <u>intensity</u> of the storm — the sounds roll off the tongue.
4) <u>Internal rhyme</u> and <u>assonance</u> are also used to give a feeling of <u>power</u> and <u>intensity</u>, e.g. "bang...vanish...flap /...black-/ Back".

Storm in the Black Forest (Pages 14-15)

1) Many of the words in this poem <u>build up a sense</u> of the storm through their <u>sound</u>. Some of them are <u>onomatopoeic</u>, e.g. "flutters", "cackle". Others are <u>alliterative</u>, e.g. "<u>s</u>till... <u>s</u>nake... <u>s</u>pilled / ... <u>s</u>ky".
2) These <u>build on</u> the very <u>visual descriptions</u> of the "bronzey soft sky" to give us a <u>real</u> and <u>complete sense</u> of what it's really like to be caught in the storm.

You can write about language features in all poetry...

'Spellbound' uses alliteration to sound like a spell. The narrator of 'Crossing the Loch' uses one or two phrases from Scottish dialect, e.g. "blaeberries", to show us some of her personality.

Section Four — Poetry Techniques

Irony

I'm not being ironic when I say this page is a real corker...

1) It's <u>ironic</u> when <u>words</u> are used in a <u>sarcastic</u> or <u>comic</u> way to imply the <u>opposite</u> of what they normally mean. People often do this to draw attention to something funny or odd.
2) It's ironic when there's a <u>big difference</u> between what people <u>expect</u> or hope for and what <u>actually happens</u>.

Irony can be a Subtle Way to Deliver A Message

A Vision (Pages 20-21)

1) The poem tells us that people <u>once</u> made <u>enthusiastic plans</u> for a <u>better</u> and <u>brighter future</u>. These plans were for the <u>perfect modern town</u>, where <u>model citizens</u> would lead <u>happy</u> and <u>contented lives</u>.
2) But the irony is that the plans were just "sketches, artists' impressions" — too <u>far-fetched</u> and <u>dreamlike</u> to ever come true. The future <u>didn't</u> turn out the way people hoped. The <u>real lives</u> of real people <u>spoilt</u> the dream.
3) In truth, people are much <u>more likely</u> to consign their rubbish to a "landfill site" — just like the future plans — than recycle it "at the bottle-bank".
4) The poet seems to think that the planners <u>didn't</u> take <u>reality</u> into account when coming up with their schemes — which is <u>why</u> they <u>didn't work</u>.

Neighbours (Pages 28-29)

1) Being "<u>neighbourly</u>" is all about <u>friendship</u> and <u>sharing</u>. The fact that "Now we are all neighbourly" could be a cause for <u>celebration</u> — something to be proud of and <u>pleased</u> about.
2) But in the years following the <u>Chernobyl disaster</u>, being neighbourly in <u>Europe</u> also meant <u>sharing</u> the <u>after-effects</u> of the accident too — a terrible <u>irony</u>.
3) The poet suggests that it was also <u>ironic</u> that at the time of Chernobyl, the government was introducing policies like Glasnost which would make the country more <u>democratic</u> — undoubtedly a <u>good thing</u>.
4) But she writes that "the <u>virus</u> and the <u>toxin</u>" are also democratic, <u>infecting</u> everyone <u>fairly</u> and <u>equally</u> without <u>discrimination</u>.

It was ironic that Kate had chosen today of all days to go to the beach.

Irony is sometimes More Obvious

Storm in the Black Forest (Pages 14-15)

1) When the narrator talks about "the electricity that man is <u>supposed to</u> have mastered", he's <u>poking fun</u> at the commonly held notion of man <u>controlling nature</u>.
2) This idea seems <u>ridiculous</u> in light of how <u>out of control</u> the storm is.
3) He's obviously being very <u>sarcastic</u>.

Some other poems contain irony...
The irony in 'The Moment' comes from the contrast between someone feeling secure and content with life (first stanza) and the harsh reality of realising they're not secure at all (second stanza).

Section Four — Poetry Techniques

Mood

There's no need to get in a mood, this section's nearly over...

> 1) Mood is simply the <u>feeling</u> or <u>atmosphere</u> in a poem.
> 2) It might be <u>funny</u>, <u>sad</u>, <u>thoughtful</u>, <u>sinister</u> etc.
> 3) Mood <u>doesn't</u> necessarily stay the <u>same</u> all the way through a poem.

Sometimes poems have a Nostalgic Mood

The Wild Swans at Coole (Pages 6-7)

1) The mood in this poem is thoughtful and nostalgic — and a little bit sad.
2) This nostalgia is created through the narrator's reminiscing and his references to change and the passing of time: "The nineteenth autumn has come upon me".
3) The sadness comes partly through the implied contrast between the swans' youth, beauty and freedom and the narrator's situation — old age has come upon him and he's lost what they have. This makes the mood quite poignant.
4) The mood makes it easier for the reader to understand and empathise with the narrator's feelings.

Sometimes the Mood Changes

The Prelude (Pages 8-9)

1) The mood at the start of the extract is mostly happy and light.
2) But the mood changes suddenly and dramatically with the line "When, from behind that craggy steep...", becoming serious and troubled. It becomes a bit philosophical, as the narrator seems to consider his own mortality, "in grave / And serious mood".
3) This change in mood helps us to empathise with the narrator's feelings more easily.

Jokes about his hair did little to improve Mike's mood.

Cold Knap Lake (Pages 24-25)

1) The poem begins with sharp, clear memories and descriptions of resuscitating the drowning child. The mood is thoughtful, but confident — "The child breathed, bleating / and rosy".
2) But the poet suddenly begins to question the reliability of these memories and the mood changes, becoming vague, dreamlike and a little bit unsettling — "Was I there? / Or is that troubled surface something else".
3) This dramatic change is surprising and its effect is to make the reader question their memories too.

All poems have a mood...

The mood in 'The Blackbird of Glanmore' is sad and thoughtful in places, but happy in others. The mood in 'Crossing the Loch' also changes as the narrator recounts her feelings about the trip.

Section Four — Poetry Techniques

The Poetry Exam: Unit Two Overview

If you're following Route A of the AQA English Literature course, you'll have to do an exam called Unit 2: Poetry Across Time. That's what this page is all about.

Your Exam Will be Split Up Like This

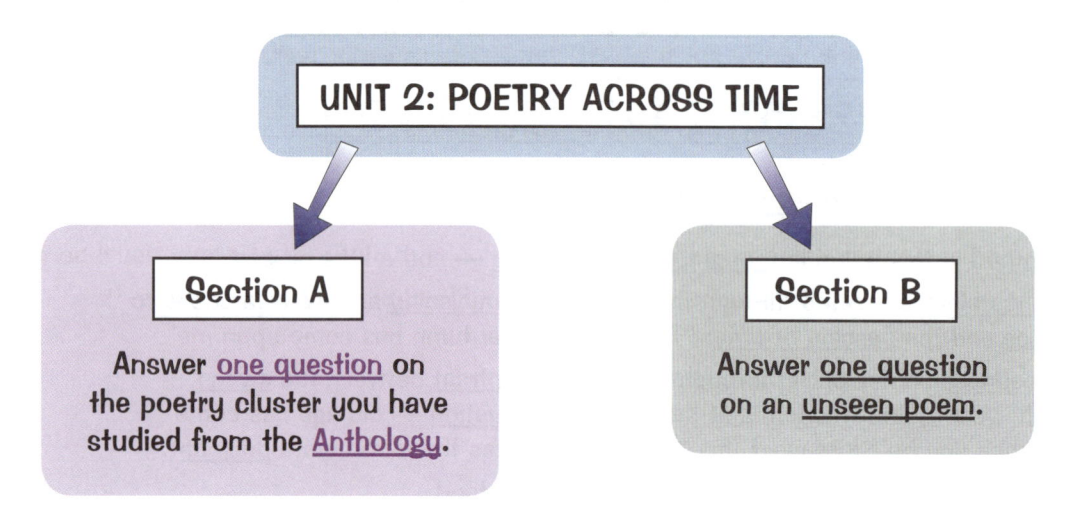

UNIT 2: POETRY ACROSS TIME

Section A — Answer one question on the poetry cluster you have studied from the Anthology.

Section B — Answer one question on an unseen poem.

1) This guide contains all the poems from the 'Place' cluster of the Anthology — this should be the one you've studied in class. There are three other poetry clusters, which you don't need to worry about.
2) The next few pages will give you tips on how to answer the question in Section A.
3) Section A is worth two-thirds of the marks in the exam and nearly a quarter of your entire GCSE.

This is How Your Exam Will Work

1) The whole exam lasts 1 hour 15 minutes. You should spend about 45 minutes on Section A. The other 30 minutes should be spent doing Section B.
2) Section A has a choice of two questions for each poetry cluster. You should only answer one question and it should be about the cluster you've studied. The question is worth 36 marks.
3) You're not allowed to take your own anthology or any notes about the poems into the exam. You'll be given a blank copy of the anthology to help you with your answer.
4) You'll also be given a separate answer book to write your answer in.

There are Instructions on the Front Page of the Exam

1) You must read the front page of the exam paper before you start — it tells you exactly what to do.
2) There will be a list of things you need for the exam. Make sure you've got everything on it.
3) Check you've got the right exam paper — it should be the one for the higher tier.
4) Remember to fill in all the details on the front page of the answer booklet.

I hope you're paying attention — there's an exam on this...
I like pages like this. Absolutely no learning whatsoever. Lovely. Don't worry if you forget some of this stuff — there'll be a reminder of how the exam works on the front page of the exam paper.

Section Five — The Poetry Exam

Sample Question 1

OK, so now you know what the exam's about. I bet you're just dying to find out what the questions will be like, eh? Er, well... Here's your first sample question anyway.

Read the Question Carefully and Underline Key Words

1) You'll have a choice of two questions, so it's best to read them both through carefully first. Then pick the one you think you've got the best chance of answering well.

2) Once you've done that, read the question you've chosen through again. Underline the question's theme and any other important words.

3) The question will give you the title of one poem and ask you to compare it to one other poem of your choice. Pick another poem you think relates to the theme.

4) Look up the poems you're going to write about in the blank copy of the anthology you'll be given in the exam. Turn over the corners of the pages they're on so you can find them again quickly.

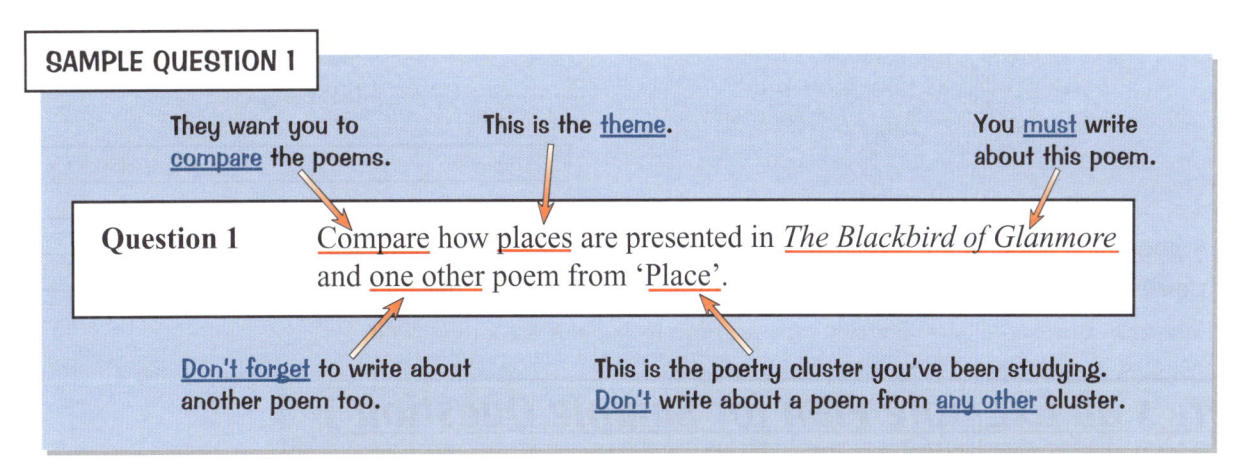

SAMPLE QUESTION 1

They want you to compare the poems. →
This is the theme. ↓
You must write about this poem. ↓

Question 1 — Compare how places are presented in *The Blackbird of Glanmore* and one other poem from 'Place'.

↑ Don't forget to write about another poem too.
↑ This is the poetry cluster you've been studying. Don't write about a poem from any other cluster.

There are Three Main Ways to Get Marks

Whichever question you choose to answer, you'll get marks for:

1) Giving your own thoughts and opinions on the poems and supporting them with quotes from the text.
2) Explaining features of form, structure and language.
3) Describing the similarities and differences between poems.

Keep these three things in mind when you're writing and planning your answer.

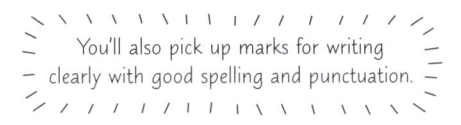

In 18th century Scotland, the penalty for forgetting to include quotes was severe.

You'll also pick up marks for writing clearly with good spelling and punctuation.

Read the question carefully...

If only I'd always followed that particular piece of advice myself — there might never have been that unfortunate incident with the policeman and the chocolate orange. Still, we live and learn.

Section Five — The Poetry Exam

Planning

If you were to ask me what my best tip would be for getting great marks in your exam, I would not say "bribe the examiner". Oh no. That would be wrong. I'd say "plan your essay answers".

Spend Five Minutes Planning Your Answer

1) Always plan your answer before you start — that way, you're less likely to forget something important.
2) Write your plan at the top of your answer booklet and draw a neat line through it when you've finished.
3) Don't spend too long on your plan. It's only rough work, so you don't need to write in full sentences. Here are a few examples of different ways you can plan your answer:

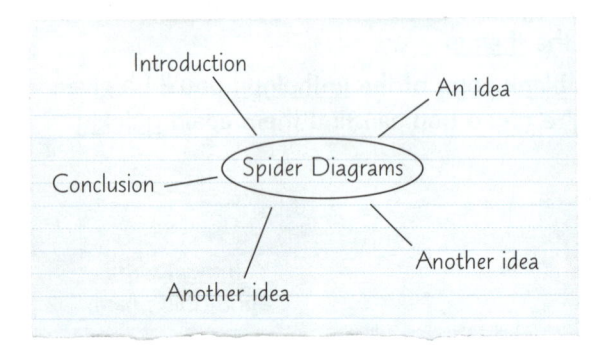

Spider Diagrams — with Introduction, An idea, Another idea, Another idea, Conclusion

Bullet points with...
- Intro...
- An idea...
- The next idea...

Tables with...

A point...	Quote to back this up...
Another point...	Quote...
A different point...	Quote...
A brand new point...	Quote...

4) A good plan will help you organise your ideas — and write a good, well-structured essay.

Here's an Example Plan for Sample Question 1

Here's a possible plan for Sample Question 1. When you're writing your plan, remember to keep in mind the three main ways to get marks from p.55. And keep it brief.

Plan: poem 1 = The Blackbird of Glanmore, poem 2 = The Wild Swans at Coole

1) Introduction — feelings about place in both poems
- Poem 1 — happy to see home and familiar blackbird, thoughtful about life and brother's death
- Poem 2 — admires beauty of place & swans, thoughtful about life / losses

2) Language Comparison
- Poem 1 — evocative lang. — "stillness dancer", "Haunter-son"
    — contrasts bring brother to life, but emphasise loss
- Poem 2 — nostalgic lang. also emphasises loss
    — "brilliant creatures... my heart is sore", contrasts between self and swans

3) Form and Structure Comparison
- Poem 1 — regular form, gives time to contemplate, circular structure
- Poem 2 — regular form, takes time to describe, circular structure

4) Wider Ideas Comparison
- Poem 1 — contrast between life and death, bird reminds him of his brother
- Poem 2 — nostalgic thoughts about life passing by, reminded by seeing swans

5) Summary — love for the places described in both poems, but also sadness

Use your plan to start making links between the poems.

Jot down any good quotes you want to use.

Don't forget to write about language, form and structure.

Write about ideas and attitudes too.

You can't write a great essay without a good plan...

This is time well spent — five minutes spent planning your answer in an exam will help you get a much better mark. Practise by planning your own answers to the sample questions in this guide.

Section Five — The Poetry Exam

How to Answer the Question

Here's an 'A' grade sample answer to the exam question on p.55.

<u>Compare how places are presented in The Blackbird of Glanmore
and one other poem from 'Place'.</u>

Introduction — 1

In 'The Blackbird of Glanmore' and 'The Wild Swans at Coole', Seamus Heaney and WB Yeats both write about places that appear close to their hearts and give them cause for contemplation. Heaney's poem begins as a happy love song to a blackbird, but soon changes to sad reflection of his brother's death. Yeats' 'The Wild Swans at Coole' is more melancholic from the start however. Although Yeats loves the swans and the parkland at Coole, he is reminded too much of his old age and the contrast between his life and that of the swans makes him sad. Both poets use contrast to explore their feelings, as well as a lengthy structure to give their poems a contemplative and thoughtful tone.

Tell the examiner how both poems relate to the theme.

It's helpful to link the poems as soon as possible.

Language — 2

At first Heaney's description of the place he is in seems upbeat; he describes the blackbird he finds upon arriving home to Glanmore as "Filling the stillness with life" and is very explicit about his feelings towards the bird: "It's you, blackbird, I love". But his tone changes, as he contrasts the happy image of the bird with that of "the house of death". Perhaps he associates his family home with death, at least in part, because of the death of his younger brother many years earlier. He continues to use contrasts, linking words together that suggest he feels his brother should not have died: "stillness dancer" suggests a lively, happy young boy, now robbed of his movement, while "Haunter-son" emphasises the loss of a much loved child, now a ghost. Yeats also uses contrasts to emphasise the feelings in his poem. The autumn scene he first describes is peaceful and serene — "the water / Mirrors a still sky" — but this peace is broken by the noisy presence of the swans, and "their clamorous wings". The swans, like the blackbird, are full of life and movement. These "brilliant creatures" not only stand out from the quiet landscape around them, they also seem to contrast with the narrator himself, who appears tired with age and claims that his "heart is sore".

Back up your points with quotes from the poem.

Talk about similarities between the two poems.

Form and Structure — 3

Heaney's poem is circular in structure; his tone is happy and light in the first stanza when he describes finding the blackbird on the grass, becoming sadder and more reflective as he begins to think about his brother's death and his own mortality: "I've a bird's eye view of myself, / A shadow on raked gravel". This change in tone is marked by the caesura of the line "Breathe. Just breathe and sit", which slows the poem right down and encourages us to contemplate with him. In the final lines, his tone becomes warm and bright again as he returns to his descriptions of the lively bird: "Hedge-hop, I am absolute / For you". His final lines also echo those at the poem's start, "On the grass when I arrive, /

Write about form and structure.

You have to write about the effect of the writer's techniques.

Section Five — The Poetry Exam

Mark Scheme

If I were you, I'd be pretty keen to find out what the examiner expected of me right about now. Oh yes, it'd definitely feature somewhere in my top 20 things to do when bored. Maybe top 50.

Look at What You Have to Do to Get Each Grade

Seriously, it's dead important to know what you have to do to get the grade you're aiming for.

Grade	What you've written
A*	• Explores several interpretations or meanings in detail • Provides carefully chosen and well-integrated quotes to back up ideas • Compares the poems thoughtfully and in detail, using plenty of evidence • Looks closely at how language, form and structure affect the reader with well-chosen examples • Gives detailed and imaginative ideas about themes, attitudes and feelings • Considers the evidence to come up with conclusions about the poem
A	• Gives several interpretations or meanings • Provides well-chosen quotes to support ideas • Compares the poems in detail and provides plenty of evidence • Describes how language, form and structure affect the reader, using examples • Looks at themes, attitudes and feelings in detail, again using plenty of evidence
B	• Thoughtful interpretation of the poems • Supports interpretations with quotes from the text • Provides some well-chosen evidence to support comparisons between the poems • Gives several examples of how language, form and structure affect the reader • Provides some evidence to support ideas about themes, attitudes and feelings
C	• Comments on several aspects of the poems, e.g. mood, language, feelings, and uses quotes to back the comments up • Makes several comparisons between the poems • Explains how language, form and structure affect the reader • Makes valid comments about themes, attitudes or feelings in the poems

You'll also be marked on your spelling, punctuation and grammar and on how you present your work. To get the best marks, your essay should be clearly organised into well-structured paragraphs. It should also be easy to follow and understand.

Section Five — The Poetry Exam

How to Answer the Question

In the ivy when I leave", bringing the poem full circle and reminding us of the bird's comforting presence. Yeats' poem also appears to have a circular structure, but while 'The Blackbird' moves from happy to sad and back to happy again, 'The Wild Swans' is a sort of mirror image, beginning and ending on a melancholy note. At first, his tone is calm and thoughtful and the mood is peaceful, but a little sad. The chaotic presence of the swans brings a livelier tone, but the calm, reflective mood returns in the final stanza when the narrator imagines the swans leaving. Unlike Heaney, Yeats ends with a sense of loss when the narrator imagines how he would feel, "To find that they have flown away".

It's a good idea to judge the poems side-by-side.

Write about differences between the poems too.

Both poets seem to have fairly complex feelings about the place they describe. For Heaney, his family home of Glanmore holds both sad and happy memories of his younger brother. The presence of the blackbird seems to lift him, transforming the place from a "house of death" to "my house of life". He loves the bird, describing its quick, quirky movements with affection: "Hedge-hop", "picky, nervy goldbeak". While the bird does make him think of his brother's accident, its lively personality also seems to remind him of the little boy himself: "Cavorting through the yard, / So glad to see me home". Yeats' place seems to contain more sadness for him than Glanmore does for Heaney. He describes things coming to an end, using words like "autumn beauty" and "October twilight". This suggests he is contemplating the end of his own life. Yeats' love for the swans is full of sadness too, because they have companionship, passion and freedom. Perhaps most significantly, they are "Unwearied still" and "Their hearts have not grown old". The constant contrasts between the swans and himself show how sad he is feeling; we can imagine that the things he feels he has lost are what the swans have — love perhaps — and because he seems old it is too late to get it back.

Try to work quotes into your sentences when you can.

Include your personal response to the poems.

Both poets seem to love the places they describe, but feel sadness too. Yeats seems particularly sad because everything he loves about the swans also reminds him of what he has lost. On the other hand, Heaney, who has lost a brother, seems able to contemplate his loss, but also celebrate the life he finds at his home in the shape of the blackbird. Perhaps Yeats has a greater feeling of sorrow because he knows the swans will ultimately leave him, and he will be alone again. Heaney, on the other hand, emphasises through the repetition of "On the grass when I arrive" that the blackbird is a constant presence; one that brings him love, happiness and most importantly "life", despite the pain he has also experienced.

It's good to end with a clear summary of your ideas.

Section Five — The Poetry Exam

**THIS IS A FLAP.
FOLD THIS PAGE OUT.**

Sample Question 2

Okey doke, here's another <u>Sample Question</u> for you — it's <u>number two</u> of <u>three</u>, you lucky thing. Have a think about how <u>you'd</u> answer it, then turn over for an <u>example</u> of how you could do it.

Here's Sample Question 2

This is another <u>example</u> of the type of question that might come up in your <u>exam</u>.
Remember to <u>read</u> the question <u>carefully</u> and <u>underline key words</u>.

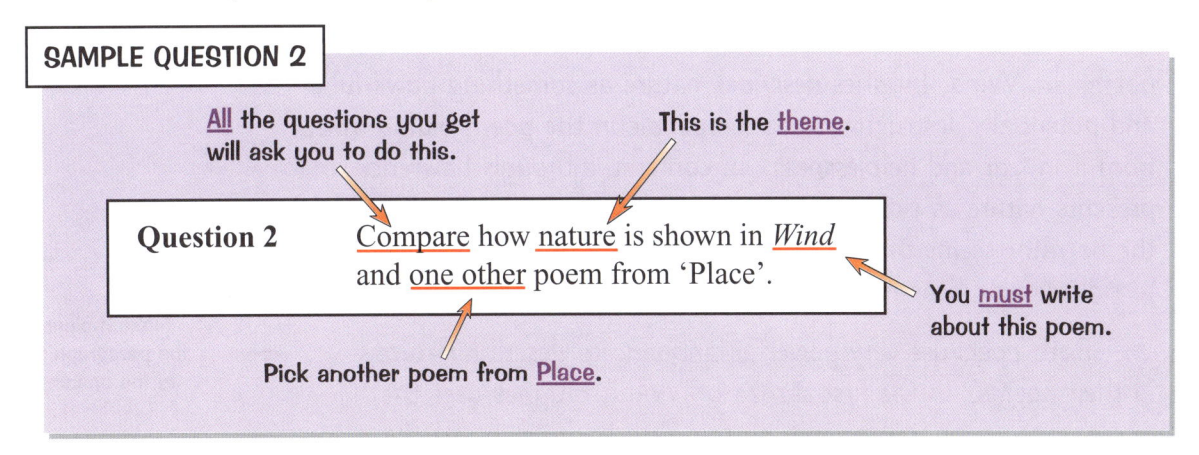

SAMPLE QUESTION 2

<u>All</u> the questions you get will ask you to do this.

This is the <u>theme</u>.

Question 2 — <u>Compare</u> how <u>nature</u> is shown in *Wind* and <u>one other</u> poem from 'Place'.

Pick another poem from <u>Place</u>.

You <u>must</u> write about this poem.

Here's an Example Plan for Sample Question 2

Here's an example of a <u>different way</u> you could plan your answer. Remember, you need to start thinking up <u>comparisons</u> between the poems at the <u>planning stage</u>.

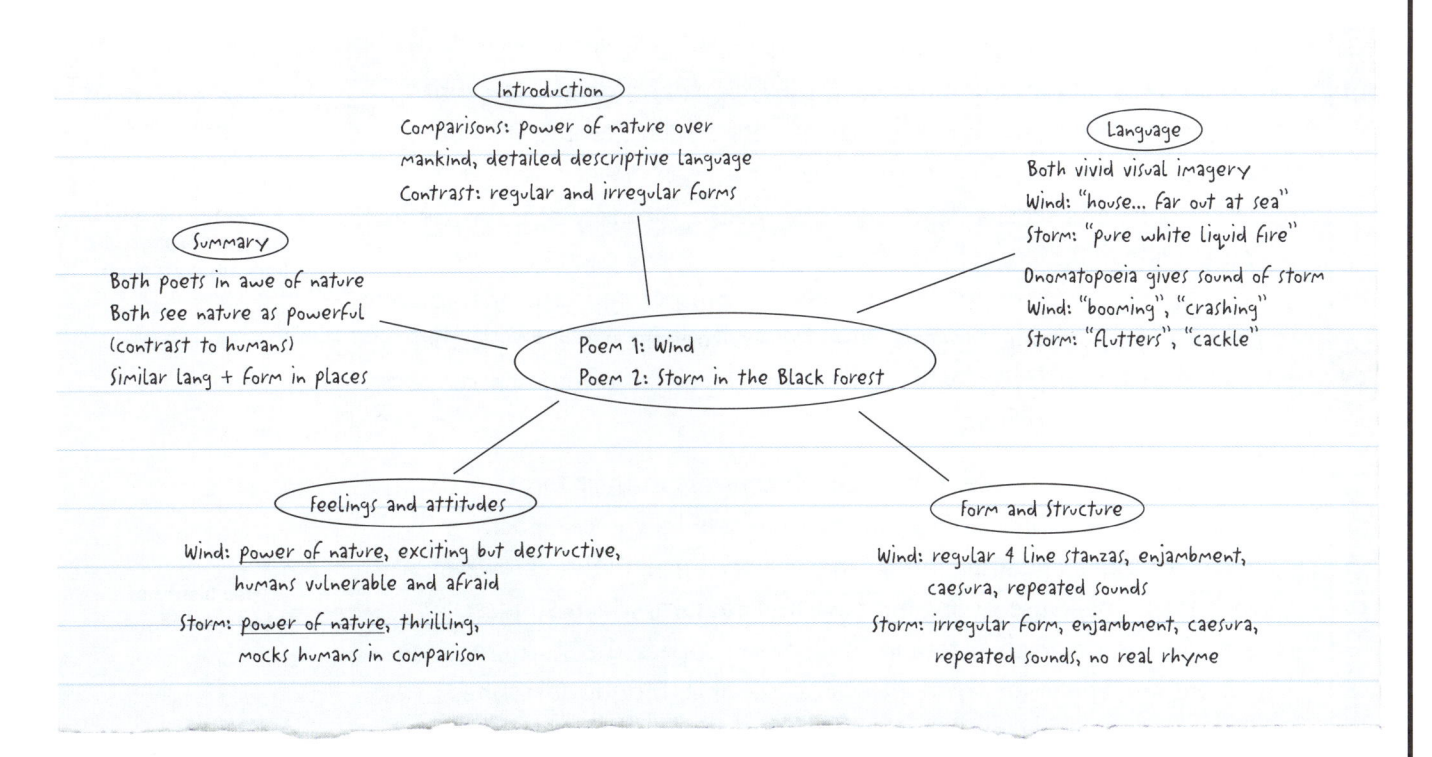

Introduction
Comparisons: power of nature over mankind, detailed descriptive language
Contrast: regular and irregular forms

Language
Both vivid visual imagery
Wind: "house... far out at sea"
Storm: "pure white liquid fire"
Onomatopoeia gives sound of storm
Wind: "booming", "crashing"
Storm: "flutters", "cackle"

Summary
Both poets in awe of nature
Both see nature as powerful (contrast to humans)
Similar lang + form in places

Poem 1: Wind
Poem 2: Storm in the Black Forest

Feelings and attitudes
Wind: power of nature, exciting but destructive, humans vulnerable and afraid
Storm: power of nature, thrilling, mocks humans in comparison

Form and Structure
Wind: regular 4 line stanzas, enjambment, caesura, repeated sounds
Storm: irregular form, enjambment, caesura, repeated sounds, no real rhyme

Try out different types of plans to see what's best for you...

When you're writing answers to <u>practice exam questions</u>, try doing your <u>plan</u> a bit <u>differently</u> each time — that way, you can work out the <u>best way</u> to <u>organise your ideas</u> before the real thing.

Section Five — The Poetry Exam

How to Answer the Question

Here's an 'A' grade sample answer to the exam question on p.59.

<u>Compare how nature is shown in Wind
and one other poem from 'Place'.</u>

Introduction — 1

Nature is presented as a very powerful force in both 'Wind' and 'Storm in the Black Forest', but is met with different attitudes in each poem. In 'Wind', Hughes describes nature as something powerful and potentially destructive, with the people in the poem hiding away from it in fear and helplessness. In contrast, although Lawrence presents nature as extremely powerful in 'Storm in the Black Forest', the narrator seems thrilled with his experience of the storm, using it to ridicule any ideas humans may have of controlling it.

Explain how the poems relate to the question.

Language — 2

Both poets use very powerful language to describe nature in their poems. In the first stanza of 'Wind', Hughes uses the onomatopoeic "booming" and "crashing" to hammer home the noise and violence of the storm, making it seem loud and terrifying. He also uses the visual metaphor of his house being "out at sea"; we can easily picture the defenceless house, completely at the mercy of nature. It suggests that the narrator feels vulnerable and afraid, an idea further developed when he later describes "the roots of the house" moving. This image suggests that everything that once seemed stable and secure no longer feels this way to him: "roots", after all, should be strong and unmovable. Lawrence's narrator also describes the power of nature, but seems much more exhilarated by what he sees, and far less threatened, than the narrator in 'Wind'. His vivid descriptions and sensual language, such as the "bronzey soft sky" and "pure white liquid fire" of the storm make the event sound mysterious and thrilling. The colours he uses give a feeling of light and magic, perhaps like lightning. He also uses onomatopoeia, for example the "cackle" of thunder, to create a poem that affects all of our senses, just like the storm must be affecting him.

Make it clear what the paragraph's about in the opening line.

Expand on your points.

Remember to compare and contrast the two poems.

It's good to have more than one example to back up your point.

Form and Structure — 3

In some ways, the poems seem to contrast in their form. Hughes has regular four line stanzas, whereas Lawrence's poem is much less rigid; line and stanza lengths vary throughout. However, both poets make use of enjambment and caesura, which suggests they are describing their feelings as they experience the storm, making it more immediate for the reader. For example, Hughes describes trying to go outside, and seeing a "black- / Back gull bent"; the break between "black" and "back" sounds as if he has had his breath snatched away for a second by the wind and adds to the feeling of

Use plenty of technical terms.

Section Five — The Poetry Exam

How to Answer the Question

threat from the storm. It reminds us just how powerful the weather is. Lawrence's use of enjambment seems to show how caught up he is in the moment. His poem has a very spontaneous feel about it; the way the lightning, "wriggles among it, spilled / and tumbling wriggling down the sky" sounds like he also is catching his breath at the power of the storm and with excitement. This is enhanced by his repetition of colours in "pure white... bright white / ...still brighter white", as if he is constantly redefining what he is seeing rather than calmly composing his thoughts after the event.

Develop your own ideas and interpretations.

It seems quite important to both poets to contrast nature with people; as if they feel that nature is so powerful it is impossible for humans to compete against it. In 'Wind', Hughes writes that "the tent of the hills drummed and strained", emphasising the immense power of the wind. If it is strong enough to affect the hills, humans do not stand a chance. The words "drummed" and "strained" are particularly effective because they both suggest tension; this echoes the feelings of the people in the house when, later on in the poem, they "grip" their "hearts" with fear, unable to do anything but "sit on" and wait for the storm to end. Lawrence is more explicit about the power of nature and how he feels humans are insignificant against it. The words "the electricity that man is supposed to have mastered" have a mocking tone, with "supposed to" suggesting that he does not believe it is possible to control such power. He ends the poem by repeating "supposed to!" on a line of its own, really emphasising his disbelief. Ending the poem on this note suggests that he is in awe of nature and that he believes the rest of us should be too.

Keep relating your answer to the question's theme.

It's good to go into detail about specific words and phrases.

Use quotes, even when you're not specifically commenting on language.

In conclusion, both of these poets feel very strongly about the power of nature. They use descriptive, vivid language to involve us in their poems effectively. However, Hughes seems to be saying that nature is threatening, whereas Lawrence celebrates nature and seems excited by its power. Despite this, the poems share similarities in their form, both of which seem to reflect the storms they describe, shown through enjambment and caesura. Ultimately, the narrator in 'Wind' is afraid of nature's power, and perhaps tries, but fails, to tame it, whereas the speaker in 'Storm in the Black Forest' feels that there is no point in trying to control nature, so embraces it instead.

Keep making comparisons.

It's good to end with a brief summary of your ideas that refers back to the question.

Sample Question 3

Here's your third and final Sample Question. You could try to come up with your own rough plan for an answer — remember, you can choose to write about any other poem you like.

Here's Sample Question 3

Not much to say here. You should know what you're doing by now...

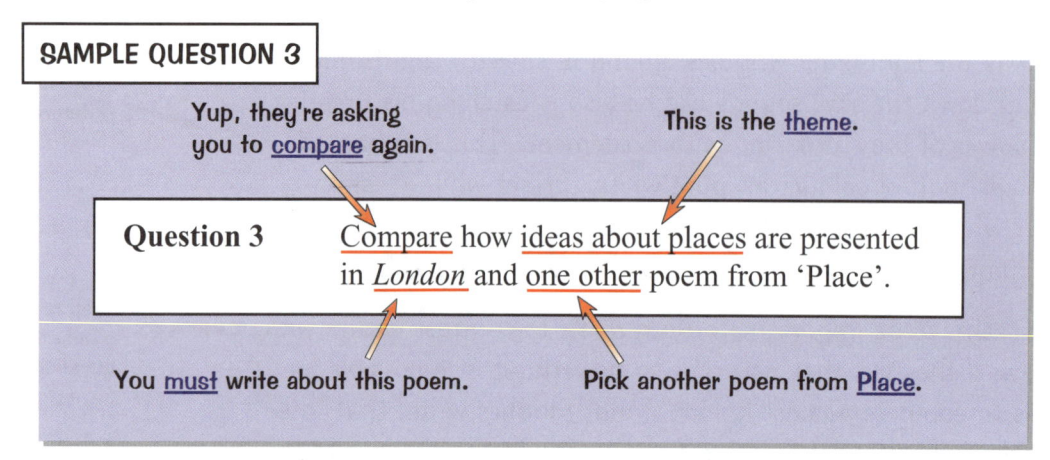

SAMPLE QUESTION 3

Yup, they're asking you to compare again.

This is the theme.

Question 3 — Compare how ideas about places are presented in *London* and one other poem from 'Place'.

You must write about this poem.

Pick another poem from Place.

Here's an Example Plan for Sample Question 3

Here's another way you could plan your answer. The table helps you sort out which quotes you want to use to support each of the points you make.

Intro
Poem 1: London, Poem 2: A Vision
Response: both poems describe somewhere urban using depressing and sometimes bitter language

	London	A Vision
Language — descriptive, urban	Angry, bitter — "mind-forged manacles" Dramatic — "blights", "plagues" Sometimes shocking — "marriage hearse"	Hopeful at first — "Cities like dreams" Unrealistic — "fuzzy-felt grass" Bleak at end — "landfill site"
Form and Structure — different	Regular rhythm and rhyme emphasise misery and drudgery Sounds like politician's angry speech	Contrasts first line, "The future was a beautiful place, once", with final line, "all unlived in and now fully extinct".
feelings and attitudes: both poems think urban landscape is bleak	Unrelenting, no hope at end, blames those in power — "each chartered street", "Every black'ning church"	No hope at end — "now fully extinct" Blames architects and planners — "neat left-hand / of architects — a true, legible script"

Conclusion
Poems written many years apart, but both think urban world is bleak / spoilt
Both use vivid imagery and lang. to present ideas / attitudes
Both suggest lack of hope for future

Always write about language, form and structure...

...but not necessarily in that order. It doesn't matter how you structure your essay as long as it:
a) makes sense, b) is easy to follow and c) covers the three main ways to get marks (see p.55).

Section Five — The Poetry Exam

How to Answer the Question

Here's an 'A' grade sample answer to the exam question on p.62.

<u>Compare how ideas about places are presented
in London and one other poem from 'Place'.</u>

1 Introduction

Both William Blake and Simon Armitage present pessimistic attitudes towards urban places in their poems. In 'London', Blake portrays the city as full of misery and despair and offers no hope for its future improvement. In 'A Vision', Armitage describes old plans for the ideal future town, but — by contrasting bleak reality with an unrealistic dream — he reveals the hopelessness of ever achieving the perfect place to live.

You can give a brief summary of what the poems are about in the introduction.

2 Language

Blake presents his attitude towards London through striking language. From beginning to end he uses dark, dramatic images to impress upon us the horror he sees on the streets around him; the pain of the "mind-forged manacles", and the corrupting influence of the "black'ning church". Some of his most emotive images contrast purity and corruption; "youthful harlot", for example, contrasts the innocence of youth with the seediness of prostitution, while the joy of marriage is haunted by death in "marriage hearse". Repetition of key words — "In every cry of every man... / In every voice" — also emphasises his message of unrelenting gloom. Armitage, on the other hand, appears to begin by painting a picture of hope and happiness, using images such as the beautiful, "cities like *dreams*, cantilevered by light". These images make the future sound like a wonderful place, but we soon realise that Armitage is using these words cynically, deliberately basing his language in fantasy — "fairground rides... executive toys" — to make the plans sound unrealistic and unachievable. Armitage emphasises this feeling with the language he uses to describe reality; the cold-sounding "north wind" and grimy, unglamorous "landfill site" contrast starkly with earlier, cosy images of "board-game suburbs" and "fuzzy-felt grass".

Use quotes to back up your points and explain them.

Use linking words and phrases like this one to compare the poems.

Try to work quotes into your sentences wherever possible.

3 Form and Structure

Form is very important in Blake's poem. It is very rhythmic and has a regular rhyme scheme of ABAB, making it sound compelling and memorable when read aloud. The rhythm brings power to the words, and it is easy to imagine Blake reading the poem as a speech. This links in to his use of other rhetorical devices, such as repetition and emotive language. His poem builds up in power until the final verse when he says "But most...". We already think the things he has described are shocking, so it is depressing that there is even worse to come. He has structured the poem so that in the final verse he uses the most powerful negative language of the poem, such as "harlot", "curse", "blasts", "blights"

Short topic sentences can be effective.

Talk about the effects of structure and form on the reader.

Section Five — The Poetry Exam

SECTION SIX — CONTROLLED ASSESSMENT

The Controlled Assessment

If you're following Route B of the AQA English Literature course, you'll have to do a controlled assessment task for Unit 5: Exploring Poetry. That's what this section is about.

This is How Unit 5 Works

1) Your teacher will set you a question on some poetry. They might decide to use poems from the poetry Anthology that's covered in this book.
2) The question will ask you to compare contemporary poems (like those in Section 2) with ones from the Literary Heritage (Section 1).
3) You might have to listen to or watch performances of the poems and write about them in your answer.
4) You're expected to write around 2000 words. Your answer is worth 25% of your final GCSE grade.

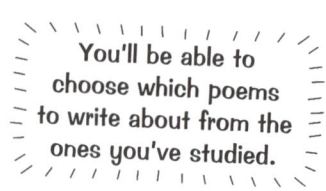

You'll be able to choose which poems to write about from the ones you've studied.

You're Allowed to Plan Your Answer First

1) You'll be able to spend time in class planning and preparing for this essay.
2) During this time, you'll be allowed to look at books and the Internet and ask your teacher questions. You must make a note of anything you use to help you (e.g. a website) in a bibliography.
3) You can write a rough draft if you want, but you won't be able to have it with you while you're writing up your answer. You can take in brief notes though.

You'll Have Up to Four Hours to Write Up Your Answer

1) You'll write up your answer in your classroom over a few lessons, but you'll be under exam conditions.

For Sam's control assessment he had to demonstrate skilful changing of channels.

2) You'll be given unmarked copies of the poems to help you.
3) You can write up your essay by hand, or type it up on a computer.

> You'll be allowed a dictionary or to use your spell-check, but if you do have a computer you won't be able to get on the Internet.

4) Your work will be collected in at the end of every session. When you've finished, your teacher will collect in everything you've written — including any drafts you did earlier on.

You'll write up the task under exam conditions...
So, your teacher will set you a question on some poems you've studied. You'll have time to prepare your answer, but you're expected to write it up in a maximum of four supervised hours.

Section Six — Controlled Assessment

How to Answer the Question

and "plagues", for maximum and lasting impact. Armitage also builds to a climax in his poem, structuring his lines so that the opening, "The future was a beautiful place, once", contrasts strongly with the conclusion that the plans are "all unlived in". This contrast emphasises how pointless the plans and dreams were, and how different reality is. The description of the plans as "now fully extinct" leaves us with no hope that reality will ever approach anything as amazing as the dream world previously described.

Explain the effects of language too.

Blake's poem seems to convey the attitude that London has become a place of despair and sadness that affects "every man" and even "every infant". Armitage's poem suggests that it was the real lives of "people like us", who use the "landfill" rather than the "bottle-bank", that did not fit in with the far-fetched dreams of the architects and planners, thus spoiling their idealised world. Both poets appear to feel anger towards those with power. Blake mentions "each chartered street" and "the chartered Thames", which might relate to those who control the city streets. Since the Thames is natural, it seems ironic that someone feels they can control it; perhaps the narrator is mocking this attitude. He also seems to feel angry with those who do not try to change things. His descriptions of the "black'ning church" and the "blood down palace-walls" are damning. Perhaps Blake feels that royalty and the church have a responsibility to help people overcome poverty and despair. Armitage's anger seems less obvious, but when he writes about the architect's "neat left-hand... a true, legible script" his tone sounds cynical. Since left-handedness is often associated with creativity, perhaps he is suggesting these planners were more interested in artistic ideas than realistic plans.

Don't forget to keep making comparisons.

Try to expand your ideas.

In conclusion, although these poems were written many years apart, they both have the attitude that their city or town is a place lacking in hope. Blake's poem has more instant impact, as he lists the dreadful sights of London, building up to a climactic final verse of misery. Armitage's poem is more subtle; at first we may even be taken in by the dreamland envisaged by planners, but the images are gradually undermined, and are shown to be too good to be true. The narrator finally fully reveals his real opinions and his bitterness is almost equal to that in Blake's poem. Both poets present negative attitudes to their town, and conclude with a tone of bleakness and bitterness.

End with a strong conclusion that relates back to the question.

Section Five — The Poetry Exam

THIS IS A FLAP.
FOLD THIS PAGE OUT.

The Controlled Assessment

I expect you'd find it helpful to know what kind of questions you're going to get asked, how best to approach them and what you'll be marked on. So I've done a nice page about it for you.

You'll Be Marked on Three Main Things

Whatever question you get, you'll get marks for doing these three things.

Keep them in mind when you're planning and writing your answer.

1. Giving your own thoughts and opinions on the poems and supporting the points you make with quotes from the text.
2. Explaining features of form, structure and language.
3. Describing the similarities and differences between poems.

This means you should always compare the poems you're writing about.

Here Are Some Example Questions

EXAMPLE QUESTION 1

Explore the different ways poets present places that are important to them in the poems you have studied.

EXAMPLE QUESTION 2

Explore how language is used to create a sense of place in a range of contemporary and Literary Heritage poems.

1) You can choose which poems you write about, but you must include at least one contemporary and one Literary Heritage poem. The number of poems you write about is up to you, but make sure you have plenty to say about each one.
2) Even though the question might not specifically ask you to compare the poems, that's what you have to do to get good marks.

Think About How You're Going to Tackle the Question

The question you get might be quite general, so you're going to have to think about the best way to approach it. You might find it helpful to start off with a basic plan like the one below.

- Choose poems which relate to the theme of the question.
- Look at the language — what effect does it create? How does it do this?
- Look at the form and structure — what effect do they create? How do they do this?
- What are the feelings and attitudes in the poems?

} How do the poems compare with each other?

Prepare your answer carefully...

The question you get is set by your teacher, but you'll always be marked in the same way. Always write about language, form and structure, as well as the feelings and attitudes in the poems.

Section Six — Controlled Assessment

The Controlled Assessment

A good plan will help you organise your thoughts and write a clear, well-structured essay — which means lots of lovely marks. And the good news is, you'll have plenty of time to prepare one.

Choose Your Poems and Map Out Ideas

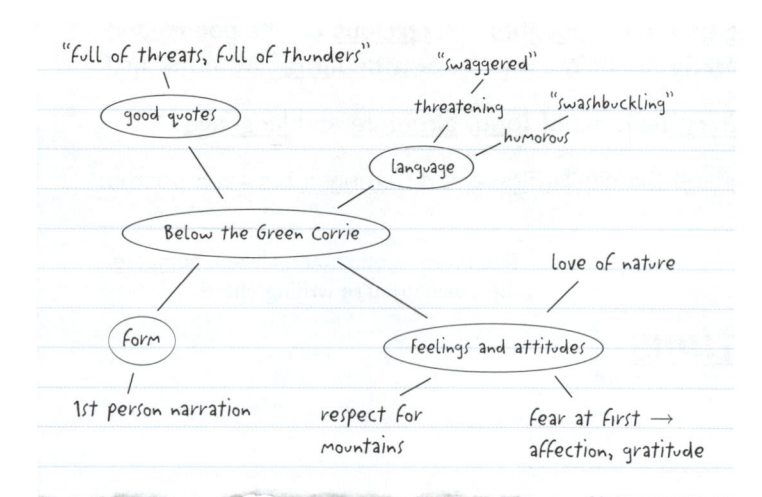

"full of threats, full of thunders" "swaggered"
good quotes   threatening "swashbuckling"
         language   humorous
Below the Green Corrie
                  love of nature
form   feelings and attitudes
1st person narration   respect for   fear at first →
              mountains   affection, gratitude

1) Let's say that for Example Question 1 on page 65, you decide to write about 'Below the Green Corrie'.

2) You might want to map out your ideas, as shown on the left, so you can decide what to include in your detailed plan.

3) It's a good idea to do this for all your poems and make links between them.

4) Write down some key quotes you want to include in your essay too.

Write a Detailed Plan

Here's an example plan for Question 1 on the last page. You can make it fairly detailed, as you've got enough time.

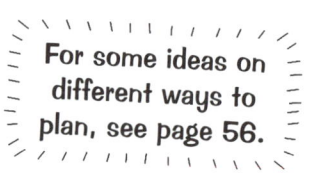

For some ideas on different ways to plan, see page 56.

Introduction
Poems: Below the Green Corrie, The Prelude, Price We Pay For the Sun and Hard Water
All significant places to the poets

Feelings and Attitudes
- Green Corrie — respect / love for mountains
- Prelude — perspective on nature changed, threatened by mountain
- Price We Pay — complicated love for islands
- Hard Water — feels defined by home town pride

Language
- Green Corrie — bandit imagery — "swashbuckling"
- Prelude — contrasts — "elfin pinnace", "grim shape"
- Price We Pay — natural imagery links island to family — "breasts / like sleeping volcanoes"
- Hard Water — qualities of water echo qualities of people and place — "Honest water, bright and..."

Form and Structure
- Green Corrie — loose rhyme / rhythm
              — sounds natural
- Prelude — long narrative structure, blank verse
- Price We Pay — informal, last lines answer title
- Hard Water — last stanza 14 lines
              — sonnet to show love for water?

Conclusion
- All poems use different techniques to present places that are important to them. All passionate about places, shown through language used.

Plan what you're going to write about before you start...

Use your preparation time wisely to come up with a good plan for your essay. You won't be allowed it with you when you're writing up, but you can have a few notes to jog your memory.

Section Six — Controlled Assessment

The Controlled Assessment

Here are some grade 'A' paragraphs from a sample answer to Example Question 1 on page 65.

Here's a Sample Introduction

Write an introduction that makes it clear you've understood the question, like this one:

> Place plays a very important role in 'Below the Green Corrie', 'The Prelude', 'Price We Pay for the Sun' and 'Hard Water'. All of these poems are about places that mean a great deal to the poets and they use a variety of techniques to present them to us. 'Price We Pay for the Sun' and 'Hard Water' are both about connections to home, while 'The Prelude' and 'Below the Green Corrie' combine reassuring and threatening images to present scenes of a life-changing encounter with nature.

Tell the reader the names of the poems you're going to discuss.

Here are Some Sample Paragraphs

You've got 2000 words to really explore the poems in depth. You don't have to write about every little bit of the poems — focus on writing about a few key elements in detail.

> 'Below the Green Corrie' and 'The Prelude' both use personification to bring the mountains they describe to life. MacCaig's bandit imagery is particularly effective, illustrating that there are two sides to the mountains. To begin with they appear threatening: they "swaggered up" menacingly and are "full of threats, full of thunders". This creates a strong sense of danger and they seem able to cause the narrator real harm. But the image is also vaguely humorous with the word "swaggering" sounding more like it should come from a film or comic. As the poem continues, the mountains are affectionately made to sound like "swashbuckling" heroes; wild but lovable rogues who also have a capacity for fun and enjoyment. They are capable of sharing their greatness; in the second stanza, we are surprised to hear that, "it was they who stood and delivered / They gave me their money and their lives". It seems they give up their strength and power to the narrator, whose life, he claims, is "enriched / with an infusion of theirs". This is a stark contrast to the "huge peak" personified in The Prelude, which robs the poem's narrator of his confidence...

Make it clear what each paragraph's about in the first line.

Back up your ideas with quotes.

Analyse the language closely.

Remember to compare the poems.

It's important to give your own opinions on the poems. Make your interpretations sound more convincing by giving plenty of evidence to support them — this means using lots of quotes.

> Although hard water may seem like an unusual choice for the subject of a poem, we quickly understand why Sprackland might have chosen to write about it. To her the qualities of the water define both the place she comes from and the people who live there, all being "Straight", "Honest" and "blunt". These qualities seem to be ones she values; she later says with pride, "It tasted of work, the true taste / of early mornings". It appears this poem is a celebration of such qualities. The poet seems to want to emphasise the unglamorous but straightforward nature of the water — and as a result the town itself — with her down-to-earth description of its "swimming-pool smell"...

Keep focused on the theme of the question.

Look at the poem's wider messages.

Give your own personal interpretations.

Section Six — Controlled Assessment

How to Write an A* Answer

It's what you've all been waiting for: absolutely everything you need to know to write an utterly fantastic, knock-the-examiner's-socks-off, quite-frankly-blummin'-amazing A* answer. Phew. Better have a cuppa first.

Know Your Texts In Depth

1) Make sure you know the poems really well — you need to be able to write about them in detail.
2) Don't just re-tell the story of the poem in your essay though — and don't try to write down absolutely everything you know about it.
3) Instead, carefully select key bits of the text and focus on writing about them in depth.

Look Closely at Language

To get top marks, you need to pay close attention to the language used in the poems.

> In the second stanza of 'Crossing the Loch', Jamie's language suddenly changes, becoming sinister and more threatening. She says "Our jokes hushed" and "I was scared"; these simple statements create a sense of fear and unease. This feeling is further enhanced by a series of unsettling images: "hunched hills", for example, and "ticking nuclear hulls". We can almost feel her start to shiver as a "cold shawl of breeze" settles around her. Personifying the hills as "hunched" and unfriendly is particularly effective, giving them power and the potential to do harm. The use of the word "ticking" is also extremely powerful; it creates a feeling of tension, as if time is passing and a bomb is waiting to go off. Because it is linked to "nuclear hulls" we fear it could be deadly.

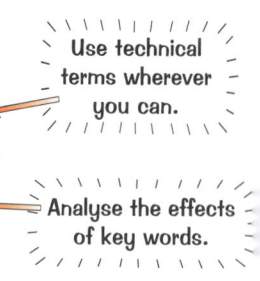

Always develop your ideas.
Use technical terms wherever you can.
Analyse the effects of key words.

Give Alternative Interpretations

1) You need to show you're aware that poems can be interpreted in more than one way.
2) If the poem's a bit ambiguous, or you think that a particular line or phrase could have several different meanings, then say so.

> On one level 'Wind' is simply a poem about a powerful, natural storm, albeit an extremely effective one. But there is evidence to suggest it has a deeper meaning. When we reach the final stanza and the ambiguous "Or each other", we begin to wonder if the poem is as straightforward as it first appears. The line seems to indicate that the couple are not speaking. Perhaps the storm is actually an extended metaphor for an argument that threatens to destroy their relationship. This would fit in with the personified wind's very human anger as it "flung a magpie away". It would also make sense that the house, described as a "fine green goblet" — a precious treasure easily broken and vulnerable to damage from the storm — is supposed to represent the troubled relationship.

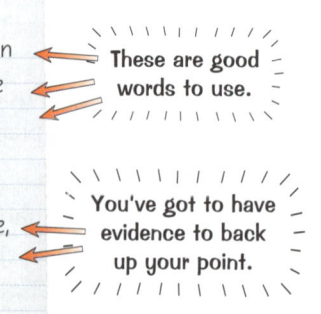

These are good words to use.
You've got to have evidence to back up your point.

3) Don't be afraid to be original with your ideas — you get marks for a personal response. Just make sure you can back up your arguments with plenty of evidence from the poem.

Give some imaginative ideas...

You could gain marks for saying something a bit different, but you must be able to support your theories with quotes — otherwise you'll look like you don't know what you're talking about.

How to Write an A* Answer

Even if your teachers aren't predicting you an A*, it's still worth looking at these pages to get a few ideas on how you could improve your work. This quoting lark for example — everyone should have a glance at that.

Always Support Your Ideas with Details from the Text

This might seem like a fairly basic point — but if you don't back up your ideas with quotes or references from the text, then you're not going to get top marks. Here are some quoting top tips:

1) Choose your quotes carefully — they have to be relevant to the point you're making.

✓ Clarke's use of the shocking image, "Crows drank from the lamb's eye", tells us straightaway that something is wrong.

✗ The narrator's fear is obvious when he says that: "And growing still in stature the grim shape / Towered up between me and the stars, and still, / For so it seemed, with a purpose of its own".

The orangey bits aren't needed.

2) Don't quote large chunks of text — it's not necessary and it wastes time.

3) Don't reel off long lists of quotes without explaining them. Remember, quotes are there as evidence to support your argument.

✗ Atwood lists the ways that nature will get its revenge: "the trees unloose", "the birds take back their language", "the cliffs fissure and collapse", "the air moves back from you like a wave". She then tells us what humans were doing to irritate nature...

This just describes what happens in the poem — there's nothing original.

✓ Atwood shocks us with the violence of nature's revenge on the arrogant humans; suddenly nature recalls everything it has given us, as "the birds take back their language" and even the very air we need to survive "moves back... like a wave". These images are both frightening and unsettling...

This is much better.

Use '...' to show when you're missing bits out.

Show Some Wider Knowledge

1) Do some research on the poems. Although you don't have to include context, it'll still look pretty impressive.

2) Don't go overboard though — your facts might be interesting, but you have to show they're relevant to your answer. It's best to keep your comments fairly short.

Heaney's description of the "lost brother – / Cavorting through the yard" may be autobiographical, his own brother having died in an accident as a young child. This gives the poem an added poignancy...

In 'The Wild Swans at Coole', the line "All's changed" could be referring to World War One and the Irish Civil War. These two monumental events would have had a massive impact on anyone who lived through them, making the world feel like a very different place. Perhaps this has added to the narrator's feelings of age and weariness.

Wider knowledge — sounds dangerous to me...

Quotes. Can't live with 'em, can't live without 'em as I believe the saying goes. Or a saying anyway. Think carefully about which ones to use and where, that's my advice. Sorted.

Section Seven — How to Write an A* Answer

How to Write an A* Answer

It's not just <u>what</u> you write that gets you an A* grade, it's <u>how</u> you write it. Show some <u>finesse</u> with a <u>tip top vocabulary</u> and a lovely <u>flowing</u> writing <u>style</u>.

Use Sophisticated Language

1) To put it simply, your writing has to sound sophisticated and stylish.
2) It should be concise and accurate, with no vague words or waffle.
3) It should also show off an impressive range of vocabulary.
4) Make sure it's appropriate though — don't use words if you don't know what they really mean.

Style and sophistication are Eddie's watchwords.

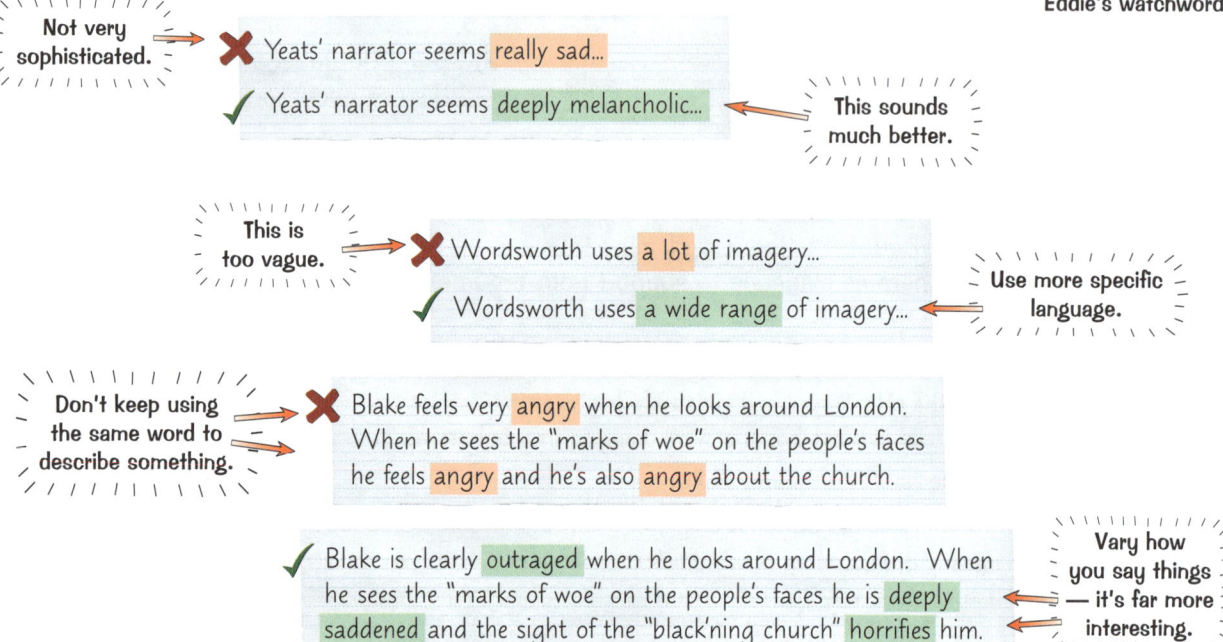

Not very sophisticated. → ✗ Yeats' narrator seems really sad...

✓ Yeats' narrator seems deeply melancholic... ← **This sounds much better.**

This is too vague. → ✗ Wordsworth uses a lot of imagery...

✓ Wordsworth uses a wide range of imagery... ← **Use more specific language.**

Don't keep using the same word to describe something. → ✗ Blake feels very angry when he looks around London. When he sees the "marks of woe" on the people's faces he feels angry and he's also angry about the church.

✓ Blake is clearly outraged when he looks around London. When he sees the "marks of woe" on the people's faces he is deeply saddened and the sight of the "black'ning church" horrifies him. ← **Vary how you say things — it's far more interesting.**

Use Technical Terms Where Possible

At A* level, you need to use the correct technical terms when you're talking about poetry. There's a handy glossary at the back of this guide that explains a lot of these terms for you.

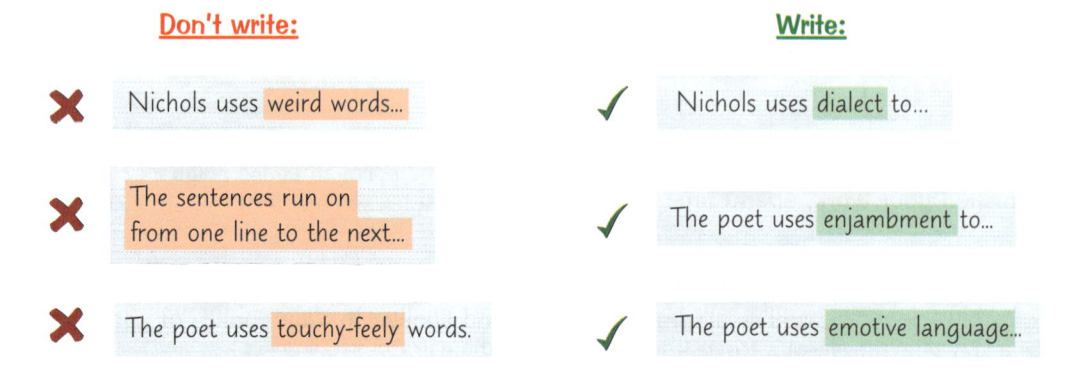

Don't write: | **Write:**

✗ Nichols uses weird words... | ✓ Nichols uses dialect to...

✗ The sentences run on from one line to the next... | ✓ The poet uses enjambment to...

✗ The poet uses touchy-feely words. | ✓ The poet uses emotive language...

Think carefully about your choice of words...

You've got to sound like you <u>really know</u> what you're talking about — and the words you use to do it will make a <u>big difference</u>. This kind of writing gets <u>a lot easier</u> with <u>practice</u> — so practise.

Section Seven — How to Write an A Answer*

How to Write an A* Answer

There's <u>more</u> to writing an <u>A* answer</u> than you thought, eh? Still, we're <u>nearly done</u>.
This last page is a <u>real winner</u>, I'm sure you'll agree, so let's get cracking.

Vary Your Sentence Structures

It's important to keep your reader <u>interested</u> in what you're saying. One way to do that is to vary the <u>style</u> and <u>length</u> of your sentences. Look at these <u>examples</u>:

This is <u>boring</u> — it's dull and <u>repetitive</u>...

> The narrator's descriptions are funny. He describes the mountains as "bandits". He says they "swaggered up". This sounds like something from a comic strip. He also says they "stood and delivered". This sounds a bit clichéd...

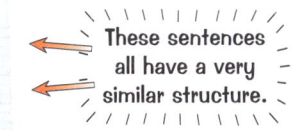

These sentences all have a very similar structure.

This is <u>varied</u> and much more <u>interesting</u>...

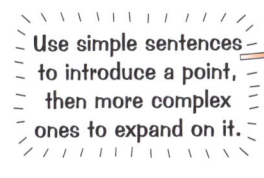

Use simple sentences to introduce a point, then more complex ones to expand on it.

> The narrator's descriptions are funny and affectionate. The mountains are portrayed as "bandits" who "swaggered up" like something from a comic strip before they "stood and delivered". The scene appears to be straight from a film: a Hollywood cliché of the Wild West...

Use a variety of punctuation, including colons (:) and semi-colons (;), when appropriate.

Your Writing Should Flow Around Your Quotes

To get an A*, your writing needs to <u>flow</u> beautifully.
This means working your quotes <u>seamlessly</u> into your sentences.

<u>For example</u>, instead of writing this...

> The narrator's descriptions of the mountain's actions are quite frightening: "Upreared its head", "Towered up", "Strode after me".

This sounds a bit awkward.

...it's much <u>better</u> to write this:

> The narrator's descriptions of a mountain that "Upreared its head", then "Strode" after him are quite frightening.

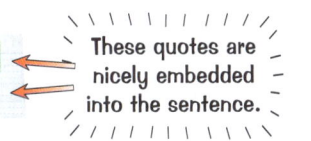

These quotes are nicely embedded into the sentence.

"Your writing should flow around your quotes like a river flows around stones."
CGP, 2010

Check Your Work

1) To get top marks, you need to avoid errors in <u>spelling</u>, <u>punctuation</u> and <u>grammar</u>.
2) Once you've finished your work, spend time <u>checking</u> it over and <u>correcting</u> any <u>mistakes</u>.
3) In the <u>exam</u>, leave yourself <u>five minutes</u> to read through your answer at the end.
   Put a <u>neat line</u> through any mistakes and write the correction <u>above</u>.
4) In your <u>controlled assessment</u>, you're allowed more time and access to a dictionary or spell-check. This means your work will be marked much more <u>strictly</u> — so check it <u>carefully</u>.

Leave time to prof-reed yuor work...

It might sound basic, but you seriously do need to <u>check your work</u> once you've finished. It's easy to make <u>silly mistakes</u> even if you're being really careful — and silly mistakes <u>don't look impressive</u>.

Section Seven — How to Write an A Answer*

Glossary

adjective	A word that describes a thing, e.g. "big", "fast", "annoying".
alliteration	Where words that are close together start with the same letter. It's often used in poetry to give a nice pattern to a phrase or create a sound effect. E.g. "The giant trees are bending / Their bare boughs weighed with snow".
ambiguity	Where a word or phrase has two or more possible meanings.
assonance	When words share the same vowel sound but the consonants are different. E.g. "past stone / past foam".
autobiographical	Describing something that happened in the poet's real life.
blank verse	Poetry that doesn't rhyme, but has a regular rhythm.
caesura	A break in the rhythm of a line.
colloquial	Sounding like everyday spoken language.
contrast	When two things are described in a way which emphasises how different they are. E.g. A poet might contrast two different places or two different people.
dialect	A variation of a language. People from different places or backgrounds might use different words or sentence constructions. E.g. In some English dialects, people might say "hey up" instead of "hello".
emotive	Something that makes you feel a particular emotion.
empathy	When someone feels they understand what someone else is experiencing and how they feel about it.
enjambment	When a sentence or phrase runs over from one line or stanza to the next.
first person	When someone writes about themselves, or a group which includes them, using words like "I", "my", "me" and "we".
form	The type of poem, e.g. a sonnet or a dramatic monologue, and its features, e.g. rhyme, rhythm, metre, etc.
free verse	Poetry that doesn't rhyme and has no regular rhythm.
iambic pentameter	Poetry with a metre of ten syllables — five of them stressed, and five unstressed. The stress falls on every second syllable, e.g. "One summer evening (led by her) I found".
iambic tetrameter	Like iambic pentameter but with a metre of eight syllables — four stressed and four unstressed. E.g. "I wander through each chartered street".
imagery	Language that creates a picture in your mind. It includes metaphors and similes.
irony	When words are used in a sarcastic or comic way to imply the opposite of what they normally mean. It can also mean when there is a big difference between what people expect and what actually happens.
language	The choice of words used. Different kinds of language have different effects.
layout	The way a piece of poetry is visually presented to the reader, e.g. line length, whether the poem is broken up into different stanzas, whether lines create some kind of visual pattern.
metaphor	A way of describing something by saying that it is something else, to create a vivid image. E.g. "The tent of the hills drummed and strained its guyrope".

Glossary

Glossary

metre	The arrangement of stressed and unstressed syllables to create rhythm in a line of poetry.
monologue	One person speaking for a long period of time.
mood	The feel or atmosphere of a poem, e.g. humorous, threatening, eerie.
narrator	The voice speaking the words that you're reading. E.g. A poem could be written from the point of view of a young child, which means the young child is the poem's narrator.
onomatopoeia	A word that sounds like the thing it's describing, e.g. "buzz", "crunch", "bang", "pop".
oxymoron	A phrase which appears to contradict itself, because the words have meanings that don't seem to fit together. E.g. "fierce lovely water".
personification	A special kind of metaphor where you write about something as if it's a person with thoughts and feelings. E.g. "The mountains gathered round me / like bandits".
phonetic	When words are spelt as they sound rather than with their usual spelling. It's often used to show that someone's speaking with a certain accent.
quatrain	A four line stanza that usually rhymes.
rhetoric	Language used by the poet to persuade you of a particular point of view.
rhyme scheme	A pattern of rhyming words in a poem, e.g. in 'London', the 1st line of each verse rhymes with the 3rd, and the 2nd rhymes with the 4th.
rhyming couplet	A pair of lines that are next to each other and whose final words rhyme.
rhythm	A pattern of sounds created by the arrangement of stressed and unstressed syllables.
simile	A way of describing something by comparing it to something else, usually by using the words "like" or "as". E.g. "my boat / Went heaving through the water like a swan".
sonnet	A form of poem with fourteen lines, and usually following a clear rhyme scheme. There are different types of sonnets. They're often about love.
stanza	A group of lines in a poem. Stanzas can also be called verses.
stereotype	An inaccurate, generalised view of something, e.g. in 'Price We Pay for the Sun', tourists think of the islands as "picture postcards" and nothing more.
structure	The order and arrangement of ideas and events in a piece of writing, e.g. how the poem begins, develops and ends.
syllable	A single unit of sound within a word. E.g. "All" has one syllable, "always" has two and "establishmentarianism" has nine.
symbolism	When an object stands for something else. E.g. A candle might be a symbol of hope, or a dying flower could symbolise the end of a relationship.
theme	An idea or topic that's important in a piece of writing. E.g. A poem could be based on the theme of nature.
tone	The mood or feelings suggested by the way the narrator writes, e.g. confident, thoughtful.
voice	The personality narrating the poem. Poems are usually written either using the poet's voice, as if they're speaking to you directly, or the voice of a character, e.g. an elderly man.

Glossary

Index

A
A* answers 68-71
ABAB rhyme scheme 5, 11
admiration 25
alliteration 10, 51
alternative interpretations 68
analysing language 68
anger 5, 29
Armitage, Simon 20
arrogance 23
assonance 51
Atwood, Margaret 22
awe 15

B
bandits 12
beautiful language 9
beginnings of poems 46
belonging 33
Below the Green Corrie 12, 35, 36, 46, 50, 67
Blackbird of Glanmore, The 18, 38, 39, 41, 45, 49, 57
Blake, William 4
blank verse 9
Brontë, Emily 10
bullet points 56

C
caesura 19, 45
celebration 27
certainty 23
Chernobyl 29, 43
Clarke, Gillian 24, 28
Cold Knap Lake 24, 38, 40, 47, 53
confident language 9
conflict 11, 27
confusion 25
contemplative language 7, 19
contrasts 5, 7, 19, 21, 29, 33
controlled assessment 64-67
couplets and last lines 47
Crossing the Loch 30, 34, 36, 38, 45, 46, 68
cynicism 21

D
dialect 27, 33, 51
dramatic language 9, 11, 17, 23, 25
dramatic monologue 5

E
emotive images 5
enchantment 11
enjambment 13, 15, 17, 19, 25, 29, 45
enjoyment 13
example plans 56, 59, 62, 66
example questions 65
exams 54
excitement 31
exclamation marks 15

F
fear 9, 17
fearful language 9
first person narration 7, 9, 13, 17, 21, 25, 27, 31, 33, 49
free verse 13
frightening language 31
futuristic language 21

H
Hard Water 32, 34, 47, 49, 51, 67
Heaney, Seamus 18
helplessness 17
hope 29, 43
hopeful language 29
hopelessness 5
horrific language 5
how to answer the question 57, 60, 63
how to write an A* answer 68-71
Hughes, Ted 16
human failings 23

I
iambic pentameter 9
idealism vs reality 21
identity 51
imagery 13, 15, 21, 27, 50
intimate language 31
irony 21, 29, 52

J
Jamie, Kathleen 30
joyful language 19

L
language about time 7
language features 51
Lawrence, D H 14
London 4, 35, 39, 42, 44, 48, 63
loss 19
love 19

M
MacCaig, Norman 12
magical language 31
mapping out ideas 66
mark scheme 58
memories 24, 31, 38
metaphors 17, 50
Moment, The 22, 37, 40, 45, 48, 49
mood 50, 53

N
natural imagery 27
nature 7, 36, 37
Neighbours 28, 41, 43, 46, 52
Nichols, Grace 26
nostalgia 31

Index

O
onomatopoeia 51

P
passion 42
patois 27
personal language 27
personification 8, 12, 17
philosophical language 25
place 34, 35
planning 56, 64, 66
poetic devices 45
poetic forms 44
poetry exam 54
power of nature 23
Prelude, The 8, 35, 36, 40, 50, 53, 67
Price We Pay for the Sun 26, 34, 41, 47, 51, 67
pride 33
proof-reading 71

Q
quotes 69, 71

R
relationships 41
repetition 5, 11, 15, 45
respect for nature 13
respectful language 13
rhetoric 5
rhyme and rhythm 48
rhyming couplets 25, 47

S
sadness 7, 19, 39
sample answers 57, 60, 63, 67
sample questions 55, 59, 62
scepticism 15
scornful language 15
second person narration 49
sentence structures 71
similes 17
sophisticated language 70
sound effects 51
Spellbound 10, 36, 42, 45, 48
spider diagrams 56, 66
Sprackland, Jean 32
Storm in the Black Forest 14, 37, 42, 44, 49, 51, 52, 60
straightforward language 33
structure 45

T
technical language 29
technical terms 70
three main ways to get marks 55, 65

U
uncertainty 40
Unit 2: Poetry Across Time 54
Unit 5: Exploring Poetry 64

V
value of water 33
Vision, A 20, 35, 39, 43, 44, 45, 52, 63
visual language 13
vocabulary 70

W
wider knowledge 69
Wild Swans at Coole, The 6, 37, 38, 44, 53, 57
Wind 16, 37, 43, 46, 50, 51, 60, 68
wonder 25
word play 27
Wordsworth, William 8

Y
Yeats, William Butler 6

Acknowledgements

The Publisher would like to thank:

For poems:
Simon Armitage: 'A Vision' — From *Tyrannosaurus Rex Versus the Corduroy Kid* (Faber and Faber, 2007)
Margaret Atwood: 'The Moment' — Reproduced with permission of Curtis Brown Group Ltd. London on behalf of Margaret Atwood Copyright © Margaret Atwood 1998
Gillian Clarke: 'Cold Knap Lake' — From *Collected Poems* (Carcanet Press, 1997), reproduced by permission of Carcanet Press Ltd.
Gillian Clarke: 'Neighbours' — From *Letting in the Rumour* (Carcanet Press, 1989), reproduced by permission of Carcanet Press Ltd.
Seamus Heaney: 'The Blackbird of Glanmore' — From *District and Circle* (Faber and Faber, 2006)
Ted Hughes: 'Wind' — From *The Hawk in the Rain*, Faber and Faber; New Impression edition (5 Jun 2003)
Kathleen Jamie: 'Crossing the Loch' — reproduced with permission of Picador, an imprint of Pan Macmillan, London. Copyright © Kathleen Jamie 2002
Norman MacCaig: 'Below the Green Corrie' — from *The Poems of Norman MacCaig* by Norman MacCaig is reproduced by permission of Polygon, an imprint of Birlinn Ltd. (www.birlinn.co.uk)
Grace Nichols: 'Price We Pay for the Sun' — Reproduced with permission of Curtis Brown Group Ltd, London on behalf of Grace Nichols Copyright © Grace Nichols 1984
Jean Sprackland: 'Hard Water' — From *Hard Water* by Jean Sprackland, published by Jonathan Cape. Reprinted by permission of The Random House Group Ltd.
W.B. Yeats: 'The Wild Swans at Coole' — From *The Wild Swans at Coole* (Macmillan and co, 1919), reproduced by permission of AP Watt Ltd. on behalf of Grainne Yeats

For photographs:
Simon Armitage, Margaret Atwood, Gillian Clarke, Seamus Heaney, Ted Hughes, Kathleen Jamie, D.H. Lawrence, Grace Nichols, Jean Sprackland — Rex Features
William Blake, Emily Bronte, William Wordsworth, W.B. Yeats — Mary Evans Picture Library
Norman MacCaig — © The Scotsman Publications Ltd. Licensor www.scran.ac.uk

Every effort has been made to locate copyright holders and obtain permission to reproduce poems and images. For those poems and images where it has been difficult to trace the originator of the work, we would be grateful for information. If any copyright holder would like us to make an amendment to the acknowledgements, please notify us and we will gladly update the book at the next reprint. Thank you.